The Business
of Trademarks

The Business of Trademarks

A Practical Guide to Trademark Management for Attorneys and Paralegals

Carol Chadirjian

Universal-Publishers
Irvine • Boca Raton

The Business of Trademarks:
A Practical Guide to Trademark Management for Attorneys and Paralegals

Universal Publishers, Inc.
Irvine • Boca Raton
USA • 2018
www.universal-publishers.com

978-1-62734-192-9 (pbk.)
978-1-62734-193-6 (ebk.)

Typeset by Medlar Publishing Solutions Pvt Ltd., India

Cover design by Ivan Popov

Publisher's Cataloging-in-Publication Data
provided by Five Rainbows Cataloging Services

Names: Chadirjian, Carol.
Title: The business of trademarks: a practical guide to trademark management for attorneys and paralegals / Carol Chadirjian.
Description: Irvine, CA: Universal Publishers, 2018.
Identifiers: LCCN 2017950774 | ISBN 978-1-62734-192-9 (pbk.) | ISBN 978-1-62734-193-6 (ebook)
Subjects: LCSH: Trademarks--United States. | Trademark searching. | Trademark infringement. | Trademark licenses. | BISAC: LAW / Intellectual Property / Trademark. | BUSINESS & ECONOMICS / Business Law.
Classification: LCC KF3180. C34 2017 (print) | LCC KF3180 (ebook) | DDC 346.048/8--dc23.

Dedication

I dedicate this book to my mother, Rose Bajakian Chadirjian. When she became seriously ill, and inspired me to write this book. I worked from my home office while being available to care for her at the same time. She urged me to go on and told me that I became so motivated and excited about the book.

Table of Contents

Table of Authorities

Cases

Apple Inc. v. Samsung Electronics Co., Appeal Nos. 2014-1335, 2015-1029 (Fed. Cir. May 18, 2015).

Burberry Ltd. v. J.C. Penney Corp., U.S. District Court, S.D.N.Y, No. 16-00982 (March 8, 2016)

Deere & Co. v. Fimco Inc., W.D. Ky., No. 15–105, October 13, 2017, Deere & Co. v. Fimco Inc., No. 5:15-CV-105-TBR (W.D. Ky. Oct. 14, 2015).

In re E.I. DuPont DeNemours & Co 476 F.2d 1357 USPQ 563 (C.C.P.A. 1973).

In re Morton-Norwich Products, Inc., 671 F.2d 1332 (C.C.P.A. 1982).

Polaroid Corporation v. Polara Electronics Corp., 182 F. Supp. 350 (F.D.N.Y. Mar. 29, 1960).

Tiffany and Co. v. Costco Wholesale Corp., No. 13CV1041, 2015 WL 5231240 (S.D.N.Y. Sept. 8, 2015).

Wal-Mart Stores, Inc. v. Samara Bros., 529 U.S. 205, 54 USPQ2d 1065 (2000).

Other Publications

Archer, Joan K. "Enforcement of Trademark Rights on the Internet: Nuts and Bolts Tools to Help Protect Against Infringement." American Bar Association, June 2012 Regional Intellectual Property CLE. http://www.americanbar.org/content/dam/aba/administrative/litigation/

materials/2012_hot_topics_in_ip_lit/2012_aba_panel3_Enforce-ment_of_Trademark_Rights_on_the_Internet.authcheckdam.pdf.

Ball, Helena. "What is the Most Counterfeited Item in the World? The Answer Will Surprise You." Inc.com, April 29, 2016, http://www.inc.com/helena-ball/most-counterfeited-brand-will-surprise-you.html.

Dike, Annie. "With This Ring, I Thee Infringe re: Tiffany's Jewelry Trade-mark." *National Law Review*, October 16, 2015. http://www.natlawre-view.com/article/ring-i-thee-infringe-re-tiffany-s-jewelry-trademark.

Faunce, Marisa D. and Benjamin B. Reed. "What's in a Name? A Lot: Trademark and Brand Protection Strategies for Franchisors," *Business Law Today* 19, no. 4, March/April 2010, available at http://www.ameri-canbar.org/publications/blt/2010/03/04_faunce.html.

Fairer, Alana M. and David P. Miranda. "The Importance of a Comprehen-sive Trademark Enforcement Program: The Changing Tides of Trade-mark Infringement." *NYSBA Inside* 34, no. 1 (Spring/Summer 2016): 18.

Fung, Brian. "Court says T-Mobile owns the color magenta," *Washington Post*, February 10, 2014, http://www.washingtonpost.com/news/the-switch/wp/2014/02/10/court-says-t-mobile-owns-the-color-magenta/.

Gambino, Darius C. "Trade Dress Litigation: Recent Trends: The Shape (and more) of Trademarks to Come." Presentation to ABS-IPL Spring Meeting, March 27, 2015, available at http://www.americanbar.org/content/dam/aba/administrative/intellectual_property_law/2015/spring/materials/revised-trade-dress-litigation-recent-trends.auth-checkdam.pdf.

Hoeppner, John. "It sells the product by itself." Quirk's Marketing Research Review, May 2008. http://www.namequest.com/uploads/QUIRKS_PDF_FILE_JOHN_HOEPPNER_ARTICLE.pdf.

Hopkins, Julie. "The Differences Between Design Patents and Trade Dress." IP Watchdog.com, June 3, 2016. http://www.ipwatchdog.com/2016/06/03/differences-design-patents-trade-dress/id=69591/.

Igor, *Building the Perfect Beast: The Igor Naming Guide* (2017), https://www.igorinternational.com/process/igor-naming-guide_short.pdf.

International Trademark Association. "Fact Sheet: Considerations in Selecting a Trademark." Updated September 2016. http://www.inta.org/TrademarkBasics/FactSheets/Pages/ConsiderationsSelecting-TrademarkFactSheet.aspx. 9/2016

International Trademark Association. "The US Trademark Registers – Supplemental v.

Principal," *INTA Bulletin No. 9*, May 1, 2002.

Rachofsky, Curtis and Michelle P. Cotulla. "Selecting a Brand Name that Shines: Avoiding the Perils and Pitfalls," *Corporate Counsel*, April 2012, https://www.ipo.org/wp-content/uploads/2013/03/Brandnamethat-shines.pdf.

Mazumdar, Unalaska. "Trademarks/Aesthetic Functionality: John Deere Colors Might Be Aesthetically Functional," Bloomberg BNA Intellectual Property Law Resource Center with the United States Patent Quarterly (October 23, 2015).

Norambuena, Paola. "10 Most Common Naming Mistakes." Interbrand. com. http://interbrand.com/views/10-most-common-naming-mistakes/. Accessed February 21, 2017.

Rivera, Richard. "United States: Appellate Court Confirms Feature's Functionality Prevents It from Acting as Trade Dress." *INTA Bulletin* 71, no. 21 (December 15, 2016). http://www.inta.org/INTABulletin/Pages/United_States_3_7121.aspx.

Smith, Robert W. "Diligence in Acquiring Trademarks: What's Due?" *INTA Bulletin* 60, no. 11 (June 15, 2005). http://www.inta.org/INTABulletin/Pages/DiligenceinAcquiringTrademarksWhat'sDue.aspx.

Smith, Robert W. "Making Your Mark: Issues in Trademark Selection." *INTA Bulletin* 60, no. 11 (June 15, 2005). http://www.inta.org/INTABulletin/Pages/MakingYourMarkIssuesinTrademarkSelection.

Llewellyn, Paul C., Richard A. DeSevo and Kyle D. Gooch. "The Shape of Things to Come: The Benefits and Challenges of Protecting Product Configuration and Packaging Design." In Arnold & Porter Kaye Scholar LLP, *Adapting to Innovation*, 11–13. Fall 2016.

Stim, Richard. *Patent, Copyright & Trademark: An Intellectual Property Desk Reference*. 10th ed. Berkeley: Nolo, 2009.

Seraiki, James. "What's in a Brand Name?" *New Yorker*, November 14, 2016, http://www.newyorker.com/magazine/2016/11/14/whats-in-a-brand-name.

Talley, Monica Riva. "Trademark Due Diligence in Corporate Transactions," Patent Trademark and Copyright Journal, October 3, 2014, available at https://www.bna.com/trademark-due-diligence-n17179895825/.

Thompson, Stephanie. "Coldwell Banker Web Symbol Becomes Corporate Icon: Can a Golden Retriever Help Push More Real Estate?" *Advertising Age*, August 5, 2002, http://adage.com/article/digital/coldwell-banker-web-symbol-corporate-icon/35377/.

United States. *Trademark Manual of Examining Procedure (TMEP)*. Washington, D.C.: Dept. of Commerce, Patent and Trademark Office, October 2017.

United States. *Trademark Trial and Appeal Board TBMP*, Washington, D.C., Dept. of Commerce, Patent and Trademark Office, January 2017.

Watkins, Alexandra. *Hello, My Name Is Awesome: How to Create Brand Names That Stick*. Oakland, California: Barrett-Koehler, 2014. September 2014.

Wells, Nicholas D. "Trademark Due Diligence in M&A: The Steps Everyone Overlooks." The website of Kirton McConkie PC. May 21, 2015. http://www.kmclaw.com/newsroom-articles-Trademarks-Mergers-Acquisition-Due-Diligence.html.

Ziff, Elaine D., and Del Val, Grace. "IP Due Diligence in M & A Transaction Checklist, Practical Law Intellectual Property & Technology." Practical Law. 2014. us.practicallaw.com/3-501-1681Preface.

Preface

*T*he Business of Trademarks: A Practical Guide to Trademark
Management for Attorneys and Paralegals* is intended as a
practical guide for legal professionals seeking to learn about
trademark prosecution. The United States Patent and Trademark Office (hereinafter "PTO") publishes the Trademark Manual of
Examining Procedure (hereinafter "TMEP"), which is the official reference manual used by the Trademark Examining Attorney (hereinafter
"Examiner"), however, as a practical matter, it is too detailed and technical
to be useful for training purposes for someone who is new to trademarks.
The United States Trademark Association (now known as the International Trademark Association, hereinafter as "INTA") published *"Trademark Management" in 1982*, but no other comparable training guide has
been published since that time. *The Business of Trademarks: A Practical
Guide to Trademark Management for Attorneys and Paralegals* aims to fill
the gap. It will enable legal professionals or students of law to acquire the
skills and knowledge necessary to perform day-to-day trademark work
diligently, confidently and with efficiency.

Trademark law is a highly specialized area of law. Training attorneys
and paralegals in trademark law with no prior knowledge can be difficult and very time-consuming. Often corporate or litigation attorneys
and paralegals do not know much about trademark law; it is an area unto
itself. Many law firms and companies do not have dedicated trademark
departments, or even intellectual property departments. I worked at a large
firm and was the only trademark paralegal and was assigned to work with
two litigation attorneys who were given the responsibility of handling the
firm's trademark prosecution. The firm did not have a systematic training
process for bringing attorneys or paralegals up to speed on how trademark

prosecution works. As the trademark manager, training attorneys and paralegals became my responsibility. We could certainly have used a book like this!

The book is organized by first defining what trademarks are and their function and how the areas of intellectual property – trademarks, copyrights, and patents – differ. I have included a number of visual aids to define and differentiate trademarks, patents, and copyrights, in addition to, providing examples of different types of trademarks being word marks, slogans, standalone designs, and wordmark with design.

Next, I address the trademark registration process beginning with selection of a trademark, trademark searching for clearance, filing the application, proving use of the trademark, having the trademark published for opposition, acceptance of the application for registration, and issuance of the Certificate of Registration to the registrant. I also review post-registration matters, such as maintenance and renewal required to keep trademarks valid and enforcement of trademark rights for the rest of the life of the trademark, until perpetuity.

We will also cover important business considerations related to trademarks, such as corporate transactions; an important segment of trademarks often overlooked, but is pure evidence that trademarks are valuable assets. A full chapter is devoted to outlaying the role trademarks play in corporate transactions and the important preclosing due diligence process. All actions up to commercial closing are explained. The appendices provide examples of PTO forms, closing lists, and other forms to track documents throughout the process. In addition, proper use of trademarks and the use of proper trademark symbols in advertising and publications.

A wealth of resources and tools are available on the PTO website. The trademark section is divided into trademark prosecution, trademark trial and appeal board (hereinafter "TTAB") for adversarial filings, and the assignments division for recordal of assignments and other changes in ownership for trademarks and patents. Within that division there is a searchable database which extracts chains of titles. The three separate divisions of the PTO are mutually exclusive and there is no intercommunication between divisions.

Additionally, the full text of the TMEP is online. Also, searching, electronic filing, document retrieval and trademark status can be found on the site. All trademark laws and United States statutes, code of federal regulations, and the guide for identification of international classes of goods and services and appropriate language for the description of goods and services are available in full text.

Also, there are trademark training videos and other educational materials that far exceed the scope of this book.

Trademark management involves much more than merely filing applications. It has greatly expanded and involves areas such as trade dress, domain names, famous marks, marketing, packaging, and unfair advertising. The development and use of the Internet gives trademark owners a huge area that needs careful policing against not only trademark infringement, but typo squatters, cybersquatters, and counterfeiters.

It is a fascinating area of law. I have spent most my professional working life in this area because I am passionate about it. My goal is that *The Business of Trademarks: A Practical Guide to Trademark Management for Attorneys and Paralegals* will be on many bookshelves and desks of those new to trademarks that require training in trademark law in a concise, comprehensive, and understandable guide to trademark prosecution. Nothing gives more satisfaction than having the official Certificate of Registration, the U.S. government's gold corporate seal, in your hand after all the work is done!

Chapter One

Introduction to Trademarks

Basic Principles

Consumers are constantly being bombarded with brand names in the marketplace. Manufacturers are constantly creating new and improved versions of their products, with logos with new colors, motion, and sound. The constant pulse of advertising on television, on the Internet, and in printed publications threaten to make consumers jaded. In this context, brand management is a challenging endeavor. How do you create a trademark that is so memorable that whenever consumers encounter this brand, they at once think of you, the producer? How do you catch and hold the customer's attention? What branding strategies will attract customers to buy one brand over another? How can you select a trademark that represents your sterling reputation and quality products in the marketplace? How can you create a trademark suggestive enough of the product, that is still registrable? How does your brand recognition function better than your competitors? How about quality products? Inventing clever brand names and logos is critical to commercial success. But cleverness is not enough. Understanding what makes a trademark memorable is great; making a great trademark registrable and strong over time is our challenge. This is the perfect coordination of marketing and trademark management.

Many elements go into effective brand management. Creating a distinctive trademark, whether a wordmark or a wordmark with a logo requires selecting carefully chosen words to effectuate a distinctive mark with a positive connotation in the minds of the consumer that indicate the source. Trademarks are source identifiers—they function to identify and distinguish the products from one company to another. The success of a brand owner is measured by how its trademark is perceived in the eyes of the consumers in the marketplace. A strong, distinctive trademark distinguishes one owner's products from that of the competitor, while promising consistent quality, reputation, and goodwill associated with the owner. It is the trademark attorney's job to evaluate the registrability of marketing's choices for a proposed trademark. A trademark that aids in selling the product and is registrable is our goal. Trademarks protect the consumers from confusion as to the source of the goods or services.

A trademark may be a word, logo, package design, device, trade dress, sound, scent, color, or a combination thereof used in commerce to distinguish a product or service from one source to that of another source.[1]

Trademarks are most often words (word marks) and logos (design marks) or a combination of words and logo. They can also be names, personal or business, a title of a book or movie, names of fictional characters, corporate names, or domain names, provided that the trademark functions as a trademark.

Trademark rights accrue through actual use in the marketplace. This is known as common law usage. This simply means that the owner has the right to use the trademark and accrue value without the benefit of a federal registration, although a federal registration will greatly enhance the value of the trademark.

Applications must claim a basis under which they are filed. The main bases are use based or 1(a), or intent-to-use (hereinafter "ITU") or 1(b). In a 1(b) application, use of the trademark on the goods or in connection with the services must be proven prior to registration. The first use date is the earliest date that the trademark is used on the goods or in connection with the services claimed in the trademark application. Most importantly, the specimens submitted to the PTO in support of the application must show the trademark exactly as it appears in the application and as currently used on the goods or in connection with the services. It is important to be aware that, from a trademark perspective, use in commerce must be interstate, rather than intrastate and forbids merely reserving a mark that may or may not be used in the future. Trademark rights are signified by use of the mark on the goods or in connection with the services. In an application based on 1(a), the applicant already proved use of the mark in the initial application.

---

[1] Trademark Act of 1946, as amended ("Lanham Act"), 15 U.S.C. § 1051 et. seq., 1127; PTO, *TMEP* (Washington, D.C.: Dept. of Commerce, Patent and Trademark Office), October 2017.

Trade dress is another type of trademark or source identifier, and of late, this area of intellectual property law has become very litigious and news-worthy. Trade dress is a "symbol" or "device" within the meaning of §2 of the Lanham Act. Trade dress consists of a product's shape, design, color, texture, or packaging that identifies the product's source. To function as trade dress, the features of a product need to be distinctive and but not functional to the use or purpose of the product or its services. An example of trade dress is COCA COLA's shape of the classic Coca Cola bottle. The Coca Cola bottle is a splendid example of trade dress and a famous trademark combined in the same mark. The shape of Coca Cola bottle is recognized worldwide. Once consumers see the bottle, there is an immediate connection to the product and the company that produces it, the Coca Cola Company. The overall commercial impression allows consumers to connect and distin-guish the Coca Cola or Coke bottle products from other cola manufacturers.

The main function of a trademark is to be a source indicator. Trade-marks are a product of the company producing those goods or services and seek to protect consumers from the likelihood of confusion as to who the producer or manufacturer is. It is the responsibility of the Examiner to reject any trademark that has the likelihood of confusion to a trademark with prior use or priority dates.

"Famous trademarks" are given an extra layer of protection. This added protection is designed to protect the owner of a famous trademark from later users seeking to profit from another company's investment in its brand. Willful infringers aim to steal the fame and reputation of the owner, along with confusing the public as to the source. These infringers cause what is known as trademark "dilution"—the lessening of the effect of a trademark. A trademark owner's reputation and goodwill attached to its marks and are important components of a mark's value.

The Lanham Act provides that "a mark is famous if it is widely recog-nized by the general consuming public of the United States as a designa-tion of source of the goods or services of the mark's owner"[2] A famous mark is considered "famous" if it meets the following requirements:

(i)   The duration, extent, and geographic reach of advertising and publicity of the mark, whether advertised or publicized by the owner or third parties.

---

[2]15 USC § 1125(c)(2)(a).

(ii) The amount, volume, and geographic extent of sales of goods or services offered under the mark.

(iii) The extent of actual recognition of the mark.

(iv) Whether the mark was registered under the Act of March 3, 1881, or
the Act of February 20, 1905, or on the principal register.

The prohibition against conduct that dilutes a famous trademark protect famous trademark owners from subsequent users trying to profit from
the famous mark's goodwill and reputation, thus, lessening the value of
the famous trademarks creating dilution and tarnishment. "Dilution by
blurring" is the association arising from the similarity between a famous
trademark and a similar mark. Statutes states that "dilution by tarnishment
is an association arising from the similarity.... That harms the reputation
of the famous mark.

Chapter Two

Trademarks as a form
of Intellectual Property

Trademark's Relationship to Other Forms of Intellectual Property

Intellectual property is defined by the Convention Establishing the World Intellectual Property Organization (WIPO), Stockholm on July 14, 1967 (Article 2 (viii)) as:

– literary, artistic and scientific works
– performances of performing artists, phonograms and broadcasts
– inventions in all fields of human endeavor
– scientific discoveries
– industrial designs
– trademarks, service marks and commercial names and designations
– protection against unfair competition

There is much confusion about difference between the types of intellectual property. Intellectual property consists of trademarks, patents, and copyrights which are intangible assets to the company that owns it. During corporate transactions, intellectual property plays a significant part as being a valuable corporate asset. The chart differentiates between patents, trademarks, and copyrights:

A patent grants the owner a time-limited monopoly over new and original inventions, processes, or designs, or new and original updates to existing inventions, processes, or designs. There are design patents, plant patents, and utility patents. While designs may be protectable both as patents and trademarks, only patent law protects the useful or utilitarian function of an invention, while trademark law protects the nonfunctional

Different Types of Intellectual Property

	Trademarks	**Patents**	**Copyrights**
Governing Body	Patent and Trademark Office	Patent and Trademark Office	Library of Congress
Who owns them?	Businesses, individuals, government, not-for-profit organizations, or estates	Businesses, individuals, government, or inventors	Creators of works— writers, artists, architects
What do they protect?	Word, logo, word and logo, slogans, sound, smell, color, or trade dress	New or improved functional processes	Original works of authorship, artwork, productions in all mediums
What rights do they confer?	Exclusive rights of the trademark. Protection against competitors trading on good will. Ability to sue infringers	Exclusive rights to prevent others from making, using, selling, or importing the invention or design	Exclusive rights of the work. Evidence of copyright ownership of creative works and ability to sue infringers
Duration	Registrations are valid for 10 years, maintenance between 5th and 6th years and renewal at the 10th anniversary of date of registration until perpetuity	Nonprovisional patent protects inventions for 20 years without the benefit of renewal; design patent is 14 years	Endures throughout the author's lifetime and 70 years thereafter. Nonrenewable

and distinctive elements. The existence of a utility patent on a trademark indicates that it is not registrable.

Copyrights protect creative and original literary works, artwork, and music. Copyrights protect the creator's rights for a certain period. The Creator has the right to protection of the copyright, whether a copyright application is filed or not. Copyright sometimes overlaps with trademark rights. For example, the copyrighted titles of books or films can function as trademarks.

Chapter Three

Types of Trademarks

A s previously stated, a trademark is a word, combination of words or random letters, group of numbers, business name, personal name, surname, domain name, stylized lettering, a stand-alone design mark, slogan, sound, scent, or trade dress, or some combination of these elements as a composite mark. It is used to distinguish the source of a product or service from that of others.

Most trademarks are wordmarks, such as OZ in plain text or logos. Some have stylized typeface; others are slogans like PLAY ON WORDS FOR SUCCESS. A mark's lettering or logos may have sound or motion as a part of the mark. The MGM's roaring lion was one of the first sound trademarks. A logo may be in black and white or in color. When color is claimed as part of the mark, it must always be used in that color; use of a version of the mark in the wrong color will not be protected.

Another type of trademark is trade dress. Trade dress is defined as: "the total image of a product, including features such as size, shape, color or color combinations, texture, graphics, or even particular sales techniques."[3] There are two versions of trade dress, product packaging or product design. A hint as to whether it is product packaging or product design is that if there is a live utility patent registration for the trade dress sought to be registered as a trademark, the trademark is considered functional and not entitled to registration on the Principal Register. Prima facie evidence of a functional trade dress is if a utility patent exists. Trade dress will be discussed in detail in Chapter 7.

Business or corporate names can function as trademarks if the name is used about the goods and service, not merely on a letterhead or business

---

[3] *Wal-Mart Stores, Inc. v. Samara Bros., 529 U.S. 205, 54 USPQ2d 1065 (2000).*

card. Corporate names are governed by the Secretary of State's office in the state in which the corporation was formed. In the corporate section, there is a corporate name search database containing all the registered corporations formed in that state which is used to find if a corporate name is available for use. Note that the database only has records of companies that were formed or qualified to do business in the state. Many corporate entities do business in more than one state, so filing for authority to do business in a foreign state or states is required. An authorization to do business in a foreign state must be filed in each state that business is conducted in. Business names that are "doing business as" (DBA) filings may also qualify to function as a trademark if they are used on the goods or about the services for which they were created. The governing agencies for this are the county in which the business was established and the Secretary of State's office retains a copy of the records. States are only concerned with a corporate name not being used in that state only. It should be noted that trademarks and corporate entities may both be entitled to be registered as a federal trademark; the trademarks are awarded national rights.

Personal names, surnames, and signatures of persons living or deceased may be entitled to trademark protection if they are used as trademarks. This applies to both fictitious and real names, living or deceased. If an applicant is seeking to register a personal name of a living person, then written consent must be obtained to use the person's name. On the other hand, if the name is fictitious, then a statement in the application needs to be added that it is merely a fictitious name, not the name of any living individual.

Less common trademarks are certification marks and collective marks. Certification marks are used to symbolize a quality or excellence. An example a certification trademark is PC Editor's Choice which certifies a certain quality of products contained in the magazine, rather than the maker. According to TMEP §1304(b), "the purpose of a certification mark is to inform purchasers that the goods or services of a person possess certain characteristics or meet certain qualifications or standards established by another person". A certification mark does not indicate a sole source the way trademarks do. The message conveyed by a certification mark is that the goods or services have been examined, tested, inspected, or checked by an objective person or organization, who is not their producer, using methods determined by the certifier/owner. The placing of the mark on goods, or its use in connection with services, constitutes a certification by someone other than the producer that the prescribed characteristics or qualifications of the certifier for those goods or services have been met.

Collective marks are marks used to show members of a collective organization. Members of the UNITED BROTHERHOOD OF CARPEN-TERS® or Kosher Symbol U® use the marks.

A trademark that is used in connection with services, rather than products or goods, is called a service mark. The Lanham Act defines "service mark" as follows:

> The term "service mark" means any word, name, symbol, or device, or any combination used by a person, or which a person has a bona fide intention to use in commerce and applies to register on the principal register established by this [Act], to identify and distinguish the services of one person, including a unique service, from the services of others and to indicate the source of the services, even if that source is unknown. Titles, character names, and other distinctive features of radio or television programs may be registered as service marks despite that they, or the programs, may advertise the goods of the sponsor.[4]

Evidence of use of a service mark is somewhat different than a trademark. Service marks use must be shown on the services described in the application for the benefit of someone other than the manufacturer. Acceptable specimens showing use of the service mark on the services are advertising, promotional, marketing or materials from the website showing the nature of the services. It should be noted that a mere domain name does not qualify as a trademark, unless the services provided are clear and the applicant provides information so that consumers may order the services. It cannot be for a service to be used in the future.

---

[4]*Lanham Act, 15 U.S.C. §1127.*

Chapter Four

Trademark Selection

Selecting an effective trademark for a product or service is a critical part of successful branding. A strong trademark has many features. It is easy to remember, spell, and pronounce. It creates a memorable impression in the minds of consumers, it is a source indicator, differentiating its products and services from those of competitors and hopefully carrying the positive connotations of the owner's good will and reputation for quality, dependability, and consistency. A strong trademark is flexible, allowing for expansion into related goods or services or even movement into different business areas. It is also legally protectable. Choosing a strong and distinctive trademark is key to success of a brand. It can represent many things about its owner and its business. What is the persona of the company? What promises of quality, reputation, and delivery are present in the brand? Can the brand comfortably expand into related or unrelated goods or services? These are some questions that should be answered when selecting a trademark.

Trademark selection is the process by which a word, phrase, logo, or other potential trademark is identified for possible use in connection with a branding effort and evaluated for possible trademark registration. This process combines trademark law and marketing management. Potential trademarks often are pre-screened by a branding agency and rated for registrability prior to being sent to a trademark attorney for clearance.

Sometimes, trademark names are created in the attorney's office. As a trademark searcher, I was often asked to search 10 or 20 possible trademarks for a company and the final trademark was selected as the one most favored with the least risk.

If a trademark is also a corporate or business name, it is even more important because that can mean the difference between a successful company and a distressed company. Changing a corporate name is simple, but when the name is also used as a trademark and the name needs to be revised or abandoned, could lead to a huge loss for a company. When a corporate name runs into trademark trouble, the consequences are a massive rebranding effort.

Choosing Potential Trademarks

An example of a suggested naming process is as follows:

- Taking into account that which would not be registrable by the PTO.
- Consider the trademark portfolios of your competitors to see what they are using.
- Develop a list of possible marks that are both remarkable and registrable.
- Consider how the mark will be perceived.[5]

Statutory Bars Against Registration

The Lanham Act provides specific bars against registration at the PTO; it will not register marks that:

a) are immoral, deceptive, or scandalous matter;

b) consist of the flag, coat of arms, or insignia of the U.S., state or municipality, or foreign nation;

c) consist of a name, portrait, or signature identifying a living individual;

d) are confusingly similar to others on the same or related goods or services;

e) is merely descriptive, deceptively misdescriptive, or geographically descriptive or misdescriptive;

f) is merely used as a surname; or

g) if the mark is a trade dress that is functional.[6]

---

[5]Igor, *Building the Perfect Beast: The Igor Naming Guide* (2017), igorinternational.com/process/igor-naming-guide_short.pdf.

[6]Lanham Act, 15 U.S.C. § 1052.

Of these statutory bars, items (a) through (d) are absolute bars meaning that under no circumstances would the trademarks be registrable. Items (e) and (f) are often successfully arguable in favor or registration.

Strategies for Developing Strong Trademarks

Trademarks have different degrees of protection, from the strongest to the weakest:

- Fanciful or coined terms receive the strongest trademark protection. EXXON® and KODAK® are examples of strong coined terms. Neither trademark is a word with a dictionary definition.
- Arbitrary marks tend to be almost as strong as coined terms consisting of one or more real words, but their use is in connection with products or services are not related to their dictionary definition. For example, APPLE® is an arbitrary mark in connection with computers. Another example is BLACKBERRY® for smartphones.
- Suggestive marks are less strong than arbitrary marks. They are trademarks that relate to an attribute, quality, or characteristic of the product or service. Examples of suggestive marks include AIRBUS for airplanes and TOMTIT for a trademark textbook.
- Descriptive marks tend to be quite weak, and often are not registrable. They merely describe the goods or services and generally cannot be protected on the Principal Register, unless filed under Section 2(f). Descriptive marks cannot be registered if they are nondistinctive. An exception is made for descriptive marks that have longstanding use or that have acquired distinctiveness through the branding efforts of their owners. There is sometimes a very fine line between suggestive and descriptive trademarks.
- Generic marks are broad categories of goods or services that are not registrable. An example of a generic mark is CARS or NOTEBOOKS.

The pyramid below shows the hierarchy of trademark protection with the strongest at the top down to the weakest protection on the bottom.

One way to create a memorable, protectable mark is to use distinctive words and avoid descriptive or common terms. The strongest trademarks

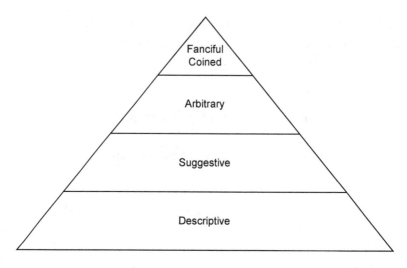

are often distinctive, coined, or arbitrary, words or phrases. If a mark or term is commonly used, it may be a weak trademark in terms of trademark value. If there are many marks with the same name, then the mark may co-exist without problems, but the protection given to the trademark will be weak. A "suggestive" trademark infers or connotes something about the mark's product or services, but does not describe them.

The PTO will reject a proposed trademark if it consists solely of simple, common terms that only describe the product or service. Descriptive words or phrases are not registrable as trademarks unless the owner can establish a secondary meaning. For descriptive trademarks to be registrable, they must attain distinctiveness either by a) showing that consumers recognize it as an indicator of the trademark's owner, resulting from a heavy investment in advertising and promotion, or b) by transferring to the Supplemental Register and after the trademark has been registered for 5 years, it is said to have acquired distinctiveness and is eligible to be transferred to the Principal Register. Using a descriptive word or phrase is a more complex and risky path to establishing trademark rights, and there is always the risk that the PTO examiner will consider the trademark to be descriptive and issue an office action refusing registration. As with descriptive words and phrases, generic terms also cannot be registered as trademarks, unless the generic term is combined with an adjective.

To be registrable, the proposed trademark should not look, sound, or feel the same as or similar to an existing trademark that is registered for use or in common law use on the same or similar goods or services, or create the same or similar commercial impression of a famous mark in any classification.

Another consideration is whether the brand will be sold in foreign countries. Cross-border branding has become more common with the development of the Internet. The translation of the brand and what it evokes in other languages and cultures is very significant. Linguistic considerations are necessary to avoid problems when the owner seeks to register the mark in other countries and that term has no negative connotations in American English or could have deeply negative meaning in other cultures or when directly translated to other languages. Searching the term in foreign languages is recommended to ensure that the name does not provoke undesirable feelings in the minds of the average consumer in target markets.

Domain names are another important consideration when designing a brand. Suitable domain names might be available for registration. Because a domain name can also serve as a trademark, it can increase the strength of the mark.

Large corporate entities often use the services of a branding agency to develop their possible trademarks. A branding agency's strategy considers the marketing and registrability of the new trademark. The aim is to create a trademark that is worthy of strong protection and serious branding efforts. A branding agency's naming team identifies several possible trademarks and uses a prescreening process to rate the candidates according to their potential for registrability and infringement of existing marks. At this early stage, the screening is not sufficient to be relied upon for clearance purposes, but is intended to identify marks that are viable for further analysis. Once strong candidate marks are identified, an attorney reviews the marks and selects the most registrable choices for preliminary or "knock out" screening by a trademark paralegal.

Chapter Five

Trademark Searches and Clearance

Trademark Searching

The importance of a thorough trademark screening process cannot be over-emphasized. Not performing a trademark search before using a mark in commerce or filing an application is risky, costly, litigious, and just plain foolish. Never do it! If a new brand is created and production, advertising, and marketing commences, it is a fundamental problem if a conflicting mark is already in use and has priority. A registrant for the application to register the new mark must be abandoned, and all the work, production, marketing, and promotion using the new, conflicting mark must be pulled and discarded. This costly mistake can be avoided by proper trademark clearance prior to filing an application.

This chapter will explain how a preliminary search is performed. The specific connectors can pinpoint or expand search results and the different situations for manipulating the number and relevancy of search results. Finally, how to review a preliminary search for direct hits and possible risks. Also, it highlights what to look for to discount a trademark or evaluate the risk of proceeding with the trademark. The contents of a full search and how to review the report is discussed. The paralegal sends a memo to the attorney highlighting the findings and possible risks involved in adopting the mark, but only the trademark attorney provides final clearance with an opinion letter to the client. Paralegals may never provide trademark clearance or any legal opinions.

The process of trademark clearance contains four steps: (1) preliminary or "knockout" search, (2) a full search, (3) reporting results and highlighting potential risks to the attorney, and (4) the attorney's opinion letter stating clearance of the trademark for registration. Performing trademark searches is a major part of the trademark paralegal's job. However, professional services firms perform the full search and create the report. Although attorneys usually do not perform trademark searches themselves, they must understand the strategies and principles of trademark searching to competently review the results of paralegal's search. A trademark attorney can suggest modifications to search strategy on a case by case basis. Following is a linear diagram showing the various stages of trademark clearance:

Step 1: Preliminary Search or Knockout Search

The search process can begin once a collection of potential marks has been made. It is common for the paralegal to be asked to search several of the marks at once in order to screen their availability. The paralegal who will perform the preliminary search needs the following information, preferably in writing, about each proposed mark:

- What is the proposed trademark name?
- Is the trademark a word mark only or will it include a design or logo? Will it be a composite mark (a mark that combines a word and a design to form a composite mark) or a standalone design?
- Are there any specific features for the mark? Unique features might include a distinctive typeset, color, design, scent, or sound.
- What is the nature of the client's business?
- What goods or services will the trademark be used for or in connection with?
- Is the trademark currently in use?
- Are there any related trademark registrations?
- Is the trademark going to be filed internationally?
- What is the desired timeframe for clearance?
- Is the trademark sought after for long-term use?
- What is the applicant's legal name and domicile as it appears in its certificate of incorporation or articles or organization and the name and title of the signatory.

The proposed marks should be entered on a chart that will track the progress of searches. The chart will include the date searches are performed. If there is a period of more than two weeks between performing the search and filing the application, then an updated search should be performed to pick up any subsequent filers.

Following is an example of a chart logging trademark searches performed:

Trademark(s) Searched	Date of Search	Results	International Classes	Goods or Services description	Who Requested Search
XYZ, ZYX, YXZ	3/3/2017	Clear	9,16,41	Financial educational materials	John Smith
XYZ, ZYX, YXZ	5/1/2017	Updated 3/2017– 5/1/2017	9	Computer programs	Cindy Meyer
YES, IT'S A GOOD IDEA	6/1/2017	X	41	Entertainment services	John Howley

A preliminary trademark search is often called a "knockout search" because the purpose is immediately rule out any exact trademarks or direct hits to quickly determine if a proposed mark can be discarded. A potential risk would be if the proposed mark, including similarity in sound, meaning, or commercial impression, and it is in use in the same or similar classes to that of the registered mark. The preliminary search looks for existing terms that are exact or confusingly similar to the proposed mark use on the same or similar goods and services. While reviewing the search, the paralegal keeps in mind any famous trademarks uncovered and tags them. If a similar mark is uncovered, the proposed trademark is off the list. Finding direct hits is a quick and straightforward way to verify that marks should not undergo any further efforts in the clearance process.

Trademark searches are performed using several tools. A firm may opt to do its searching using PTO searching database, Trademark Electronic Search System (hereinafter "TESS"), which is a basic, user-friendly search engine containing all trademarks filed with the PTO in the last 30 years, including abandoned and cancelled trademarks.[7] There are also commercial databases offered by companies like Westlaw, Lexis, and Thomson Reuters.

---

[7]TESS is accessible at http://tmsearch.uspto.gov/bin/gate.exe?f=tess&state=4805:h7nn1r.1.1

These firms offer subscription memberships for broad searching services for conducting preliminary and comprehensive searches. Preliminary searches are done in-house but full searches are performed by trademark services firms like Thomson Reuters or Corsearch. Although costly, these search firms are the elite searchers for comprehensive results with a global reach. This chapter focuses on searches using the PTO's TESS system. The site contains detailed instructions on how to perform a search, along with the variables that can be used for limitation, and the official international classifications.

1. Preliminary searches are performed as follows: Search for the exact mark, then truncated versions of the word if no direct hits are uncovered.
2. If the search returns too many hits, then limit the search by classes and/or specific goods or services. Formulate the description of goods and services as broadly as possible to include related services to pick up all potential conflicts. Consider related classes also.
3. Search the Domain Name Registry (hereinafter "DNS") for domain names that use the proposed trademark.

The TESS database includes a useful dictionary. When you enter the name of a trademark, the dictionary shows every variation of existing trademarks.

Design marks can also be searched on TESS. In a design search the proposed design is divided into the individual features of composite design. Each feature of a design mark has a corresponding 6-digit design code, which is used to perform searches for potential conflicts in the PTO database. A search can use design codes alone or can include a combination of codes and a description of the goods or services.[8] If there are 3 elements of a design, the search is treated just as a three-word trademark. Design searches are time consuming and tedious. If a preliminary search locates no hits, then a full design search should be ordered.

Here is an example of how a preliminary search might look for a standard wordmark. GREENTEAM. The proposed mark GREENTEAM can be searched as one word, *greenteam*, or as a two-word trademark *green team*. Review the results of that search. If no direct hits appear, then the

---

[8] *See* UNITED STATES PATENT AND TRADEMARK OFFICE, DESIGN SEARCH CODE MANUAL, http://tess2.uspto.gov/tmdb/dscm/index.htm.

search can proceed to the next step. The search terms need broadening to include other sounding or spelling of the terms. An example of this is *green* and *team* or *greenteam*. The addition of * around the term will uncover the term contained anywhere before or after; the * after the word would pull up trademarks that have something after the word and * in front of the term would uncover additional terms at the end of the word. An asterisk around green and team pulls up any variation containing GREEN combined with TEAM variations. To query similar sounding marks with a variation of spellings, use the syntax *(*green* or *grin* or *gren*)* and *(*term* or*tame*)*. Adding a question mark will search for one letter.

If a search returns too many hits to be practical it can be reduced in scope. The first step to reduce a search scope is to limit the search to specific goods or services with which the client proposes to use the mark. The goods and services must be described in the broadest possible terms. It is far better to include too many possibilities, then risk missing something that may be considered related. If too many hits are found and it is necessary to limit the results to marks containing the composite mark but without a long string of words that are irrelevant. Limiting by classes and/or goods or services, is an effective method to reduce the number of hits. Another method is to use proximity indicators which uncover to of the terms adjacent or limit the number of words found. The appendix contains the identification of classes and goods or services.

Here is an example of how reducing a search scope might work. Say the GREENTEAM mark is being proposed for use in connection with a magazine that will have editions in print and online. The search can be limited by adding a description of goods and services such as: *("books, magazines, publications, guides, catalog, or online services for new business startups")*. If this search still returns too many hits, the search could be further limited in scope by adding specific classes. GREENTEAM will be used in connection with Class 9 (computer programs), class 16 (publications), Class 35 (business services) and Class 41 (educational matters). Classes are searched using the syntax *IC = ("009" or "016" or "035" or "041")*. The reason for these classes is that magazines are printed publication but online should also be searched; Class 9 is the CD or computer programs, Class 35 covers business services which is the subject of the magazine, and Class 041 is added because the publications are educational.

Reviewing a Preliminary Search

It is recommended that you print full records of the same or similar marks in relevant classes or related classes up to 25 records. Related classes simply mean if you are reviewing computer programs in the financial area, then classes 9 and 36 are related. Because the media is checked in all forms. Again Class 36 is added to pick up any computer programs concerning finance. Review the trademarks found and tag exact marks and similar mark in relevant classes. Pertinent information on the record is the trademark, serial number, status, classes, goods, and applicant/registrant or last assignee and those areas should be highlighted. If a mark has been assigned, then the last assignee is owner of the mark. The record will show if the mark is still active, if the company used it as security because perhaps they are in financial trouble. If the mark is canceled or abandoned for more than the statutory period of 3 years, then it is considered dead; if less than 3 years, it could still be in use.

The criteria used to judge if a trademark would pose a conflict is generally the same as the DuPont factors:

- Is it a famous mark? In any class or classes?
- Does the owner have any related trademarks claimed?
- Is the mark the same or similar in sound, look, or feel, are its goods or services also the same or related to the goods or services of the proposed mark?
- If the proposed mark is a logo or other design mark, are the designs composed of the same elements within the composite mark? If searching for a design with five different features, if three of them are found in a trademark, then it may be a problem if the existing registration is in the same or related classifications.
- Is it a composite mark of both word and design, or a standalone design?
- Is the commercial impression similar? Does the overall or composite marks look alike.
- Are the products available in the same channels of trade and in close proximity? For example, in drug stores or high-end department stores or medical supply companies where professionals would be ordering the equipment.
- Does the registrant own related registrations?

- Are there any TTAB filings related to the mark?
- Is the owner of the mark litigiously protective of a term or mark?
- Is it a mark filed in an array of classes?
- If cancelled for less than 3 years, is it still in use?
- If unregistered, is there an office action issued and not responded to caused it to become abandoned.
- If cancelled, is the registrant still an active entity? Check the Secretary of State's website in the state it was formed in.
- Is the trademark similar to a domain name?
- Are the purchaser's professionals in the field or ordinary consumers?
- Are the two marks the same type? Is it a word mark, stylized mark, or logo?[9]

If the owner is your competitor, then a red flag should also be made on the post-it note. Another consideration if you pull up a marks that is a long slogan and it has one or two terms like the proposed mark, confusion is normally not a problem. It would be more relevant if the terms were adjacent.

When evaluating if logos are similar in a design search. The composite design or are any elements in common.

Step 2: Full Search

The professional search firms are the best at performing comprehensive searches. A full search is a bounded booklet which can be as large as 1000 pages or as small as 200. Full searches are searched in trademark (federal) and (state) databases and/or in individual countries, regions, or globally; company name searches, dba's or local business searches are searched on the Secretary of State and county levels, or globally; articles or promotional materials that are using the mark in publications or on the Internet. I have never in my career ever been asked to perform a full search but I would be competent to perform one diligently.

Review the full search report in its entirety and flag any potential conflicts. It is crucial that you take your time to pick up any possible risks. As part of the full review, print out the full records of potentially conflicting

---

[9]*In re E.I. DuPont DeNemours & Co 476 F.2d 1357 USPQ 563 (C.C.P.A. 1973).*

marks. A full record shows the entire history of the trademark, including its ownership history, whether it has been pledged as security, the dates of first use and constructive use, and other details. All records that pose a potential problem for the trademark should be tagged and pertinent information highlighted. If any of the uncovered marks are especially risky this should be noted, then a red asterisk can be added to the post-it. The same criteria are used in the full search as was used to review the preliminary search. Another very important aspect to identify the owner that has priority, either by first use date or filing date also known as the constructive use date. If the mark uncovered in the search has an earlier priority date, do not look any further.

Do not overlook the risk posed by trademarks that are marked as abandoned or expired. The statutory time for a mark to be considered abandoned is three years of nonuse. A mark that is listed as abandoned or expired on the register can still be in use even though its owner has chosen to not maintain its registration on the federal register. An abandoned application may only be temporarily in that status, for example if a response to an office action was not filed on time and is later petition to revive it is filed. It may be an excellent idea to allow time for the applicant to correct faults before concluding that the application was in fact abandoned. Perhaps the trademark was abandoned or cancelled for not filing a Statement of Use, Section 8 & 15, or Renewal. Check with the Secretary of State's office in the state where the owner was domiciled, as shown on the trademark record, to determine if the company is still in business. If the decision is made to go forward with a new registration despite the existence of potentially conflicting expired or abandoned marks, a Petition to Cancel the expired or abandoned registration can be filed to rule out any potential problems.

In a full search, also check for registered domain names that might conflict with the proposed mark. Domain names can be trademarks, but not all domain names function as trademarks. Domain names are registered on DNS, which permit new domain names to be registered so long as they are unique. The domain name registration process does not evaluate whether the proposed domain contains an existing trademark, business name, or any other factor. Consequently, many famous trademarks have been incorporated into domain names in a process called cybersquatting or typo squatting. It is therefore important that domain name searches be included in the mark clearance process. Domain names are searched using a DNS registry, such as Internic.

After review of the full search is completed, the paralegal prepares a memo summarizing the findings and pointing out potential risks. The attorney uses the information in the paralegal's memo to compile a formal legal opinion or memorandum to the client confirming that the trademark has been cleared or not.

Step 3: Clearance

Trademark clearance verifies that the proposed mark is eligible for registration and does not infringe upon any registered or pending trademarks. Once the results of a full search are received, the paralegal drafts a memo reporting the findings and any potential risks for the attorney to review. The attorney reviews the results to make a final determination that a proposed mark is cleared, meaning that the application process can proceed. Only an attorney can make this determination. The attorney delivers the summary, either as a legal opinion (typical for firm-client relationship) or as a formal memorandum (typical of in-house situations) to the client. Based on the attorney's opinion, the client can decide to go forward with the registration process. Without trademark clearance, the owner cannot in good conscience claim that no other party has a superior claim to the mark. An attorney who signs a declaration in connection with a registration application commits perjury if the application fails to disclose in good faith any existing marks that are the same or similar to the mark, and in use on the same or related goods or services, that is the subject of the application. If the examiner doesn't reject the application, the owner of the pre-existing mark can demand that the later filer stop using the mark, which can be causing thousands of dollars, time, effort, and wasted staff hours. There are options available if this situation arises: significantly amend the description of goods and services to be different in some way, limit the scope of coverage of the trademark geographically, or as a last resort, appeal to the existing registrant to negotiate a side-by-side agreement or concurrent use application where both are permitted to use the trademark, with limitations as to use. Contacting the registrant is risky. The risk is that the registrant may not agree to co-exist through a concurrent use procedure. One the other hand, Examiners tend to favor such agreements between the parties, provided that the agreement is legally correct.

Chapter Six

The Trademark Registration Process

The trademark registration process has clearly defined stages. The linear diagram shows the stages beginning with the filing of the application through registration.

Trademark prosecution is the process of obtaining a federal registration, filing maintenance and renewal applications. The process of trademark registration is illustrated by the linear diagram which explains the passage through stages of registration. Note that for a 1(a) application no Statement of Use is required because use of the mark preceded the filing of the application, so it was proven on the application.

The trademark application is assigned to a trademark examining attorney (hereinafter "Examiner") for examination. Examination of the use based application takes place, and if acceptable, then the trademark is published in the Official Gazette which is a weekly online trademark publication that publishes pending marks for opposition purposes, if no oppositions are filed, the Notice of Allowance issues and the mark is registered; an ITU application has an added step that once the Notice of Allowance issues, the owner must prove use of the mark on the goods or in connection with the services. Once accepted, the mark is registered.

In some cases, there is an added step. If the Examiner finds fault with the application, then an office action will be issued and a response is due within 6 months that will make the required changes or argue in favor of the registration Sometimes, the correction is minor and other times the rejection is substantive in nature. Once the response is accepted, the mark progresses to registration. If the Examiner issues a rejection on a final Office Action, then the only recourse is to file an ex parte appeal.

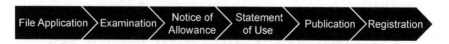

A federal registration on the Principal Register affords the registrant the following rights:

- Incontestability in certain circumstances;
- Barring imports by Customs;
- Protection against counterfeiting;
- Prima facie evidence of validity and exclusive right to use;
- Right to use the ® symbol or its textual variations, "Registered in the U.S. Patent and Trademark Office" or "Reg. U.S. Pat.& Tm. Off.,"
- Protection of a famous mark from dilution;
- Priority date for foreign filings under the Paris Convention; and
- Improved registrability of other applications with the same mark

Registration on the Supplemental Register has the following benefits:

- Right to use the ® symbol or its textual variations, "Registered in the U.S. Patent and Trademark Office" or "Reg. U.S. Pat.& Tm. Off ".
- Benefit of priority date in foreign filings of member countries; and
- Bars subsequent filers from registration.

Trademark Application

The first step in the registration process is to file a trademark application. There are two trademark registers. The Principal Register is where established marks exist; Supplemental Register is for marks that are not presently registrable on the Principal Register due to being nondistinctive or descriptive. Unlike registrations on the Principal Register, a registration on the Supplemental Register is not prima facie evidence of exclusive ownership, is not published and cannot be based on an intent to use.[10]

---

[10]INTA "The US Trademark Registers—Supplemental v. Principal," *INTA Bulletin* 67, no. 9, May 1, 2012.

A trademark application must claim a basis under which it is filed. There are several types of bases:

- Use based, 1(a);
- Intent-to-use, 1(b);
- Madrid Protocol international registration ("66(a)"); and
- foreign application ("44(d)" or "44(e)").

The applicant must also claim which international classes and offer a description of goods and services that the trademark is being used for. The TMEP contains a list of the international classification of goods and services. Sometimes the description of goods calls for an addition of a class. For example, if XYZ is a manual, then it may be in CD form (Class 9), print form (Class 16) and educational services (Class 41). A trademark in the financial services is in Class 36, but if the product is a reward program within a bank, then Classes 35 and 36 should be claimed.

The PTO's Trademark Electronic Application System (hereinafter "TEAS") website contains all the online prosecution forms. Filing online is beneficial because the applicant receives immediate confirmation of the filing, a file date and serial number. The serial number is later used to check the status of the application. It is the responsibility of the applicant to check on the status of the application every few months. Applicants are expected to do their due diligence in monitoring pending applications. If an Office Action issued but not received and the deadline for responding is past, the Examiner will then abandon the application for failure to file a response and nonreceipt of the Office Action is not a defense. The applicant has a duty to check the status of all filings with the PTO.

The prosecution division contains all the forms required to obtain a trademark registration; TTAB division contains suggested forms for adversarial filings; and the Assignment Division contains all forms to record an assignment. It should be noted that these 3 divisions of the PTO are separate and mutually exclusive. If filing a recordal of assignment or adversarial document, copies of the filings need to be sent the Examiner.

Most of the information required to fill in the form was requested at the time of the preliminary search. You use the exact name of the applicant because if the name is incorrect, then the application will be abandoned. In the case of a logo, you must file the jpg image in black and white or in color depending on whether the applicant is claiming that color is part of the mark. An accurate first-use date must be obtained for applications based on use. For trademark purposes, the first-use date is the earliest date that the product or services was made available for sale in interstate commerce. This date is very significant because it creates a priority date predating the filing date of the application and prevents subsequent infringing filers from claiming priority. Also needed is knowledge on whether the trademark has any special features, if a surname or the name of a real person, if it is being applied for as a concurrent use application. In each case, a required statement found on the form should be claimed.

Once the application is drafted and reviewed by the attorney, it is submitted electronically to the signatory. The signatory is usually a corporate officer in the application is a corporation, member or manager of a limited liability company, partner of a partnership, or the attorney of the firm handling the trademark registration. After signed, it is sent back to the preparer of the application to be electronically filed at the PTO.

Once transmitted, the trademark is immediately assigned a serial number and filing date on the confirmation copy sent back to the filer. The serial number is like a social security number—it is hereinafter the formal identification of the application and can be searched on the PTO database for status or history. The requirements for obtaining a serial number are (1) the trademark, (2) the full legal name of the applicant or owner, (3) the trademark's international classifications, and (4) description of the goods or services that the trademark will be used in connection with.

Applicants must pay a filing fee and include a declaration signed by an authorized signatory or attorney of record.

Examination

This is the period where the Examiner examines the application for registration. A trademark search is performed on the trademark to determine if it is clear. Also, the Examiner checks to make sure all required items in the application are present. The application is rigorously reviewed to see if any of the statutory bars of registration are present. If so, the Examiner will issue an office action. An office action is an official correspondence explaining why the trademark in not registrable. There may be some minor issues like reclassifying international classifications or amending a description of goods. These are very simple to correct. On the other hand, if Examiner determines that a statutory bar to registration exists, then that is a substantive action requiring the applicant to submit arguments in favor or the registration. This is very time-consuming and costly. The applicant could decide to abandon the application or prove that the trademark is in condition for registration, once these items have gone away.

Office Actions

If, however, the Examiner finds fault with the application, then an office action is issued allowing the applicant the opportunity to make the necessary changes or submit arguments in favor of its' registration. Sometimes the Examiner requires supporting documentation for a minor objection; in other cases, the refusal to register is among the bars to registration. The Examiner will explain the reason for rejection of the application and suggest possible amendments. Minor objections are very simple and quick to file. The substantive refusal is not. Refusal to register is very serious rejection on occurring because on the bar to registration have been violated. Sometimes the Applicant can submit evidence or argue in favor of the registration but it is a time consuming, costly route. The Applicant's attorney arguing in favor of the registration must examine caselaw and statutes to back up the trademark's registrability. The office action explains in detail, using caselaw, statutes, records from trademark searches and related materials that provide evidence to support the Examiner's rejection. When an office action is received, the first thing to do is to docket the deadline for filing a response within six months from the date of the Office Action. This means that at any time prior to that 6-month deadline, a response must be filed or the application will be automatically abandoned. It is important that copies be made for paralegal and attorney.

When reviewing the Office Action, it is imperative that you highlight the issues and what is required so that nothing is omitted when preparing the response. Determine if the response will need any supporting document, if so, make sure to request them as soon as possible. Another helpful suggestion is to note the cited cases and statutory references. Read the cases and relevant statutes cited. As you gain experience in responding to office actions, these cases and statutes will be cited again and again and you will become very familiar with these cites.

The next step is for the trademark paralegal to discuss the response with the supervising attorney. Then the paralegal will draft the Response to Office Action. Obtain any evidence or signatures for attaching to the response, if required. There may be an amendment to the goods description and the client needs to approve such changes. The applicant may need to supply the attorney with information or documentation to support the response to office action. The attorney then reviews it for any revisions and then it is ready to be filed.

In the case of an Office Action issued with procedural issues, a response can usually be file right away. It is advisable to do so because then the application will progress and there is no need to wait for the six-month period to be nearly over. Some of the issues are that the application may require are adding or deleting a class, an additional filing fee, requesting a substitute specimen, revising the language of the description of goods or services, adding a claim to a related registration, adding written consent to use a person's name, a question as to the ownership of the mark, the signatory was the authorized signatory being an officer of a corporation or member of a limited liability company, or the partners of a partnership.

Examiner may issue a substantive issue and there will be a refusal to register the trademark. These office actions which are serious rejections that are more complicated to overcome. These type of office actions are a refusal to register based on one of the statutory bars to registration under the Lanham Act which are itemized below. Note that items (a) through (d) in the list are absolute bars, while items (e) and (f) are subject to argument. The statutory bars are as follows:

> [N]o trademark by which the goods of the applicant may be distin-
> guished from the goods of others shall be refused registration on the
> principal register because its nature unless it—
>
> (a) Consists of or comprises immoral, deceptive, or scandalous
> matter; or matter which may disparage or falsely suggest a connec-
> tion with persons, living or dead, institutions, beliefs, or national
> symbols, or bring them into contempt, or disrepute; or a geographi-
> cal indication which, when used on or in connection with wines or
> spirits, identifies a place other than the origin of the goods and is

first used on or in connection with wines or spirits by the applicant on or after one year after the date on which the WTO Agreement enters into force with respect to the United States.

(b) Consists of or comprises the flag or coat of arms or other insignia of the United States, or of any State or municipality, or of any foreign nation, or any simulation thereof.

(c) Consists of or comprises a name, portrait, or signature identifying a living individual except by his written consent, or the name, signature, or portrait of a deceased President of the United States during the life of his widow, if any, except by the written consent of the widow.

(d) Consists of or comprises a mark which so resembles a mark registered in the PTO or a mark or trade name previously used in the United States by another and not abandoned, as to be likely, when used on or in connection with the goods of the applicant, to cause confusion, or to cause mistake, or to deceive: *Provided,* That if the Director determines that confusion, mistake, or deception is not likely to result from the continued use by more than one person of the same or similar marks under conditions and limitations as to the mode or place of use of the marks or the goods on or in connection with which such marks are used, concurrent registrations may be issued to such persons when they have become entitled to use such marks as a result of their concurrent lawful use in commerce prior to (1) the earliest of the filing dates of the applications pending or of any registration... Use prior to the filing date of any pending application or a registration shall not be required when the owner of such application or registration consents to the grant of a concurrent registration to the applicant. Concurrent registrations may also be issued by the Director when a court of competent jurisdiction has finally determined that more than one person is entitled to use the same or similar marks in commerce. In issuing concurrent registrations, the Director shall prescribe conditions and limitations as to the mode or place of use of the mark or the goods on or about which such mark is registered to the respective persons.

(e) Consists of a mark which, (1) when used on or in connection with the goods of the applicant is merely descriptive or deceptively misdescriptive of them, (2) when used on or in connection with the goods of the applicant is primarily geographically descriptive of them, except as indications of regional origin may be registrable under section 1054 of this title, (3) when used on or in connection with the goods of the applicant is primarily geographically deceptively misdescriptive of them, (4) is primarily merely a surname, or (5) comprises any matter that, as a whole, is functional.

(f) Except as expressly excluded in subsections (a), (b), (c), (d), (e) (3), and (e)(5), nothing herein shall prevent the registration of a mark used by the applicant which has become distinctive of the applicant's goods in commerce. The Director may accept as prima facie evidence that the mark has become distinctive, as used on or about the applicant's goods in commerce, proof of substantially exclusive and continuous use thereof as a mark by the applicant in commerce for the five years before the date on which the claim of distinctiveness is made. Nothing in this section shall prevent the registration of a mark which, when used on or about the goods of the applicant, is primarily geographically deceptively misdescriptive of them, and which became distinctive of the applicant's goods in commerce before the date of the enactment of the North American Free Trade Agreement Implementation Act. A mark which would be likely to cause dilution by blurring or dilution by tarnishment may be refused registration. A registration for a mark which would be likely to cause dilution by blurring or dilution by tarnishment, may be canceled.[11]

In a substantive office action, the Examiner states the reason for rejection of the application. The office action will contain the statutory cite for rejection or refusal to register and search results from TESS, citations of the relevant section of the Lanham Act, and citations of caselaw. The burden is on the applicant to nullify the rejection by submitting a response refuting these allegations and arguing in favor of the registration. All evidence must be attached to the form for filing.

A very serious, yet common rejection is a section 2(d) rejection based on the mark being deemed confusingly similar to an existing registration or pending application If the applicant has the earlier filing or use date, then the marks should be compared side to side. The DuPont factors are relied upon for this analysis. It is good practice to look at the cited owner's trademarks.

---

[11]Lanham Act, 11 USC 1052.

The trademark may be a core, longstanding mark that is very strongly protected against infringers. It may be that the registrant owns related registrations. Determine if the marks are wordmarks or logos or a combination of the two. See if the terms of the marks are similar and if the goods or services are related. Compare the dominant terms of the mark, overall commercial impression. Are the products sold in the same markets? Is the customer the average consumer or a professional in the field? If a logo is involved, examine similar features with the same rationale. Check the status of any cited registrations to see if they are active and whether a Section 8 & 15 or Renewal has been filed. If the mark has been canceled for 3 or more years, the PTO automatically considers the registration invalid. This entails finding out which state the company was formed in and searching the state's Secretary of States corporate records. If the entity is cancelled or expired then it is no longer doing business; if the cancellation or expiration has been for more than three years, it is safe to say the mark owned by them is now available. An Internet search should be sufficient to see that the mark is no longer valid. The mark's owner might have materially altered it and filed a fresh application. If the cited trademark is no longer active, then a Petition to Cancel the registration to formally nullify the registration and a copy is attached to the Response to Office Action. Argue that the marks are significantly different and should be allowed. Another alternative is to amend the goods with specificity. If there are many marks with the root are registered and argue in favor of coexistence. If there are other marks with the same root word, then the marks are successfully coexisting and are weak marks.

Determining whether two trademarks are confusingly similar can be a complicated process. One landmark case regarding a 2(d) refusal is *in re E.I. DuPont DeNemours & Co.*[12], which established factors to be considered when judging whether two trademarks are confusingly similar enough to justify a 2(d) refusal. The DuPont factors are:

1. The similarity or dissimilarity and nature of the goods or services as described in an application or registration or in connection with which a prior mark is in use.
2. The similarity or dissimilarity of established, likely-to-continue trade channels.

---

[12]476 F.2d 1357, 177 USPQ 563 (C.C.P.A. 1973).

3. The conditions under which and buyers to whom sales are made, i.e., "impulse" vs. careful, sophisticated purchasing.
4. The fame of the prior mark (sales, advertising, length of use).
5. The number and nature of similar marks in use on similar goods.
6. The nature and extent of any actual confusion.
7. The length of time during and conditions under which there has been concurrent use without evidence of actual confusion.
8. The variety of goods on which a mark is or is not used (house mark, "family" mark, product mark).
9. The market interface between applicant and the owner of a prior mark:
   a. mere "consent" to register or use.
   b. agreement provisions designed to preclude confusion, i.e., limitations on continued use of the marks by each party.
   c. assignment of mark, application, registration, and good will of the related business.
   d. laches and estoppel attributable to owner of prior mark and indicative of lack of confusion.
10. The extent to which applicant has a right to exclude others from use of its mark on its goods.
11. The extent of potential confusion, i.e., whether *de minimis* or substantial.
12. Any other established fact probative of the effect of use.

If an applicant has a pending application with related registrations, then the mark is considered strong. Thus the registrant has strong rights to the mark. An applicant of a trademark with related registrations for the same mark or root word has a stronger claim on the trademark. The Examiner evaluates the similarity of marks by comparing them side by side, rather than dissected into their separate elements. The trademark's overall commercial impression is extremely important in a 2(d) rejection. To overcome this objection, the owner must submit any related, valid registrations owned by the applicant to show a strong connection between the applicant and the trademark in question. A weaker but sometimes successful strategy is to check the TESS records to see how common the mark is. If there are many of the same marks for similar goods or about similar services, then it could be argued that the marks can safely co-exist. If that is the case, the trademark is very weak.

Sometimes the parties choose to execute a side-by-side or co-existence or concurrent use agreement and attach it to the response. Concurrent applications are allowable because of the agreement between the parties and the fact that there is some difference to the marks. This option runs the risk that the registrant will reject the proposal to enter into the agreement, and may take steps to oppose the new application. If rejected, then the owner waits for the mark to be published and opposes it then. It brings the matter to the attention of the owner. On the other hand, if the parties agree to execute an agreement, the PTO gives considerable weight to a properly drafted side-by-side agreement, but the agreement must contain all required provisions.[13]

After reviewing the records for the same or similar goods or if the mark is famous, the paralegal or attorney prepares a response providing evidence and case law supporting the claim. If the arguments submitted are accepted, then the application proceeds. If not, then the Examiner will issue a final rejection. If the applicant does not wish to abandon the application but instead decides to contest the final rejection, then an ex parte appeal with the TTAB.

Another common ground for rejection is the 2(e) statutory bars against trademarks that are merely descriptive. A mark is merely descriptive if it only describes the nature or attributes of the goods or services in question. If the applicant already owns a registration for the same or related mark, for example in other classes, then the problem can be addressed by submitting the existing registration with the response to the office action. If not, the applicant must submit arguments that the mark is suggestive, rather than descriptive. A suggestive mark is registrable, where a descriptive mark is not registrable on the Principal Register. This means that the mark suggests or connotes a connection to a point or characteristic of the mark, then the applicant can prevail. The owner must establish secondary meaning, either through 2(f) thereby amending the register to the Supplemental Register so that once registered for five years, the registration can be transferred to the Principal Register. In some cases, the applicant can submit evidence to show that it has made large expenditures for advertising and promotion of the mark, so that it has already acquired secondary meaning.

---

[13] See *In re Bay State Brewing Co.*, No. 95826258 *(TTAB Feb. 25, 2016)*.

Publication Period

If the application is in order, then the trademark is published in the Official Gazette, a weekly periodical, allowing a registrant or applicant of a pending application with priority pre-dating the published application, the opportunity to oppose to the registration of the trademark because their registration will be damaged by the published mark's registration. The publication period lasts 30 days so the registrant must file the opposition or extension of time to file an opposition within 30 days of the date of the Official Gazette that published it.

If a party wishes to oppose a registration, it becomes an "opposer" which is the Plaintiff's position in litigation. Unless an extension of time is granted, it must file an opposition within 30 days of the publication date with the TTAB. Typically, an opposer requests an extension of time to allow for research into the applicant and other trademarks in their portfolio. Once a Notice of Opposition is filed, then the Examiner puts the application on suspension until the parties agree to a solution or wait to see who prevails in this opposition. Extension may be filed up to and including 180 days.

Notice of Allowance

The PTO issues a Notice of Allowance when the application is in satisfactory condition for registration. The Notice of Allowance of a 1(b) application tolls the date for filing the Statement of Use within 6 months from the date of the Notice of Allowance. Extensions can be filed.

Statement of Use

Once the Notice of Allowance is issued, the applicant of an ITU application must file Statement of Use proving use of the mark within six months of the date of the Notice of Allowance. Note that only ITU applications require the Statement of Use; use-based applications have already proved use of the mark at the time of filing the application. The deadline is 6 months from the date of the Notice of Allowance. This deadline may be extended 4 times totaling up to 24 weeks. The first extension is automatic, thereafter extensions will be granted for cause. Failure to timely file a Statement of Use or an extension will cause the application to become abandoned.

For trademark prosecution purposes, the Lanham Act defines "use in commerce" as:

> ...the bona fide use of a mark in the ordinary course of trade, and not made merely to reserve a right in a mark. A mark shall be in use in commerce—
>
> (1) on goods when—
>
> (A) it is placed in any manner on the goods or their containers or the displays associated therewith or on the tags or labels affixed thereto, or if the nature of the goods makes such placement impracticable, then on documents associated with the goods or their sale, and
>
> (B) the goods are sold or transported in commerce, and
>
> (C) on services when it is used or displayed in the sale or advertising of services and the services are rendered in commerce, or the services are rendered in more than one State or in the US and a foreign country and the person rendering the services is engaged in commerce about the services.[14]

The Statement of Use must include a specimen showing use of the mark in interstate commerce on the goods on or in connection with the services. The required form is a digitized picture of the trademark in JPG or PDF format. If the mark is a trademark, then the specimen needs to show use on the product, packaging (such as a tag, label, or container), or display associated with the goods. For a service mark, acceptable specimens include newspaper or magazine advertising, brochures, direct-mail leaflets, menus, and business documents such as letterhead and invoices, provided that they refer to the relevant services. As with evidence of first use, specimens must have been used to on currently available products or services; they cannot merely refer to goods or services that will be available in the future. A trademark that is being used on a website for goods or in connection with services that are currently available for sale and where the

---

[14]*Lanham Act, 15 U.S.C.§ 1127.*

website provides the information for consumers to place an order, it is satisfactory to show use in commerce.

The "first use" date is the date the trademark was first available for sale. This might include the date a product is first shipped, when it is added to the applicant's website, or presented for sale at a trade show. To satisfy the interstate requirement, the method of use must be of a character that is regulated by Congress. Advertising or promotion of a product or service that will be produced or offered in the future, and is not currently for sale, will not satisfy the use requirement, nor will a brief mention on a website, unless the site sets forth how to order the product or service. Finding the earliest possible first use date or filing date is important to establish priority over potentially competing applications.

When the PTO accepts the Statement of Use, it issues an Acceptance of the Statement of Use. At this point the trademark has been approved for registration, the trademark will register in due course and the official Certificate of Registration will be sent to you.

Registration and Post-Registration Matters

Once a mark is registered it receives an official Certificate of Registration. The Certificate contains the basic details of the mark, including its registration number, date of registration, registrant's name, international classifications, and a description of the covered goods and/or services. It is critically important to carefully proofread the Certificate of Registration and that any errors are promptly corrected by filing an amendment. As soon as practical, the letter advising of the registration of the trademark and renewal date, along with marking requirements for use of the®.

The Lanham Act states that once a mark is registered the registrant must give notice to the world that they own a federally registered trademark.[15] The registrant should add the ® symbol or "Reg. U.S. Pat. & Tm. Off." to their marks. In any suit for infringement, a registrant that has failed to give such notice of registration cannot recover profits or damages. Note that the

---

[15]Id at *§1111*.

® symbol may only be used with a federally registered trademark. Use of the symbol in connection with an unregistered mark is fraud. Unregistered marks use the ™ symbol instead.

The registration date tolls the deadline for filing an Affidavit of Continued Use (hereinafter "Section 8 & 15") and Renewal. The registrant may file a foreign application in one of the member states to the Madrid Protocol and obtain the priority of the U.S. registration date. This is also called a priority date. The original Certificate of Registration should be sent to the client; in the case of a corporation, then the Certificate is for safekeeping as an official document.

The Section 8 & 15 is filed between the fifth and sixth anniversary of the date of registration. The filing verifies that the mark is and has been in continuous use since the registration. If there was a period of nonuse, then it needs to be disclosed and explained. Example reasons for periods of nonuse include renovation of a restaurant or establishment, or a strike at a production site. A current specimen of the trademark as used on the goods or in connection with the services is attached to the document. The digitized photo of the mark in jpg filed form is sent. There is a six-month grace period for late filing of the Section 8 & 15.

Registrations must be renewed at the tenth anniversary of registration. The renewal application must be filed six months before the tenth anniversary deadline to avoid cancellations. There is a six-month grace period for a late filing. Failure to file a timely renewal results in automatic cancellation of the registration.

The registration is incontestable in certain circumstances. After 5 years of registration with no adverse filings, in certain circumstances it becomes incontestable.

Proper Use of Trademarks

To maintain trademark rights, correct marking is crucial. Optimally, it is strongly suggested that presentations be made to educate other departments, such as marketing, advertising, public relations, and related departments that may use the trademark correctly each time. Other corporate department may be proficient in their jobs in their department, but it does not mean that other staff members do not require education on the overall use of a trademark in publishing and advertising. Lack of correct use of the trademark can aid in loss of trademark rights.

Only a federally registered trademark should use ®. One way to identify a trademark or service mark being used as a trademark without the benefit of a federal registration is ™ or ℠ at the end of the trademark as a superscript. While those notations indicate that the brand is being used as a trademark with or without filing a federal application.

It is imperative that those using trademarks in business, advertising, and promotional materials, both in print and on the Internet, be used correctly to enhance strength of the trademark.

Chapter Seven

Navigating the PTO Website

There is an enormous amount of information available on the PTO website on trademarks. The website contains all U.S. laws, such as the Lanham Act, Trademark Dilution Revised Act of 2006. The PTO posts regular updates of new legal and procedural developments, so it is recommended to visit the site weekly. For those new to trademarks, there are training videos and other materials quite useful, along with review of the overall process of trademark registration, pointing out the necessary steps and timeframes. For example, the educational videos explaining the basics of trademark prosecution and tips on performing trademark searches.

The entire text of the weekly Official Gazette which is a publication that is used to review published marks for opposition purposes is online.

TESS is one of the most important tools on the PTO website. It is the trademark-searching database of all federal trademark applications and registered marks in the United States There are detailed instructions on how to search a trademark, connectors, and other methods of manipulating the results to get the specific results for your search, limiting the search by international classification and/or goods and services, ownership, or assignor/assignee searches for a competitor's trademark portfolio. In addition, an entire file history of an owner can be obtained. As far as performing trademark clearance searches, there is detailed guide on all the ways a search can be used and the strategies. The dictionary is very helpful in located all derivatives of a word mark, for example, RAIN will pull up all marks starting with RAIN, containing RAN or ending in RAIN. This type of search gives you a hint as to the number of trademarks there are using RAIN.

The database contains all electronic forms needed for filing from trademark applications to renewals. Most all filings in trademark law are made via electronic filings via TEAS. The filings are submitted directly to the signatory for signature and then returned to the filer for filing at the PTO. The main advantage, although there are many, is receiving immediate confirmation of the filing, filing date and a serial number. This is a big step forward from the paper filings, with hard specimens, postcards with proper postage affixed, and a check for the filing fee. The trademark paralegal needed to photocopy all of the elements for the file and specimens were sometimes bulky. The website contains an international classification of goods and services and description of goods or services.

The Examiners use TMEP, available on the site and updated as of October 2017 as an official PTO resource for navigating the trademark prosecution process.[16] It is a huge reference book that is used by examiners to guide their review of trademark filings. The manual goes into extensive detail, with citations to statutes and applicable cases.

The PTO has separate divisions for prosecution, Trademark Trial and Appeal Board (hereinafter "TTAB") and assignment division. Each division provides access to their respective records but each is mutually exclusive. Filings need to be sent to the prosecution division to keep the record up to date. This is especially important when recording an assignment of a trademark. It is imperative that the records indicate the correct ownership or the mark is void. In multiple assignment, it is complicated, so viewing the chain of title of the ownership of the trademark is critical.

Another advantage of the PTO website is that each of the three divisions has searchable records for the public to download. Previously, in order to obtain a file history on a trademark, the applicant or attorney needed to request it in writing and take some time until you actually received it. Today, though, a simple download printed out and the file history is in your hands immediately! That is also true of the assignment records and any TTAB filings. The trademark prosecution branch provides details regarding ongoing trademark applications through its Trademark Status & Document Retrieval (hereinafter "TSDR") tool (tsdr.uspto.gov), TARR and TESS.

---

[16]United States, *TMEP* D.C.: Dept. of Commerce, Patent and Trademark Office, 2017.

The TTAB section provides information on trademark adversarial filings. Forms for filing opposition, cancellation, and ex parte proceedings can be accessed here. Whereas file histories previously needed to be requested by mail, today you can at once retrieve an entire portfolio of a competitor online in minutes. The TTAB's records (available at ttabvue.uspto.gov/ttabvue) can be searched to determine if a mark or party has been involved in any proceedings. Performing a search of a company shows all trademarks that were or are involved in adversarial proceedings to ascertain how litigious the trademark owners is likely to be. For oppositions and other litigation before the TTAB, the Trademark Trial and Appeal Board Manual of Procedure (hereinafter "TBMP") is the counterpart to the TMEP, guiding TTAB examiners on that area of trademarks.

Another division on the website is the assignment division, whereby an owner can check whether an assignment has been recorded, who the current owner is, chain of title of the trademark and whether the company has pledged mark as a security interest. Sometimes an owner has a long chain of title that needs to be tracked and this is where the records will be.

Chapter Eight

Famous Trademarks

A lthough trademark law's primary function is to protect consumers, the special rights given to famous trademarks aim to protect the trademark owners. Unlike an ordinary trademark, which is only exclusive to its owner within a narrow scope of goods or services, a famous trademark prevents another party from using the same mark in any classes of goods or services.

It is essential that registrants protect and enforce their core brands. There are many unscrupulous individuals and deceitful companies that willfully confuse the consumers and take advantage of the trademark owner's presence, reputation, and goodwill. Sometimes, the actions will be aimed at destroying the reputation of the famous mark to something that is reputably negative, scandalous and vulgar.

The Trademark Dilution Revision Act of 2006 (hereinafter "TDRA") was created to protect owners of famous marks from having their marks diluted or tarnished.[17] TDRA defines a trademark as famous "if it is widely recognized by the general consuming public as a designation of the source of the goods or services of the mark's owner."[18] The statute provides the following non-exclusive list of criteria a court can use to determine if a trademark is famous:

1. The duration, extent, and geographic reach of advertising and publicity of the mark, whether advertised or publicized by the owner or third parties.
2. The amount, volume, and geographic extent of sales of goods or services offered under the mark.

---

[17]TDRA Act of 2006, 15 U.S.C. § 1125 (2016), Pub. L. No. 109–312, 120 Stat. 1730 (2006).
[18]*Id.* at §1125(c)(2)(A).

3. The extent of actual recognition of the mark.
4. Whether the mark was registered under the Act of March 3, 1881, or the Act of February 20, 1905, or on the principal register.

The stipulation for protection under the TDRA is that it be "likely to cause dilution...regardless of the presence of absence of actual or likely confusion, competition, or actual economic injury."[19] This means that the owner of a famous trademark does not need to prove "actual confusion" to receive protection under the TDRA.

TDRA defines dilution as "the lessening of the capacity of a famous mark to identify and distinguish goods or services, regardless of the presence or absence of— (1) competition between the owner of the famous mark and other parties, or (2) likelihood of confusion, mistake, or deception."[20]

The owner of the famous trademark is allowed the right to seek remedies against infringers who first used the infringing mark or trade name in commerce after the date of enactment of the TDRA and who (1) willfully intended to trade on the recognition of the famous mark, or (2) willfully intended to harm the reputation of the famous mark.[21] Note that for the TDRA to apply, the infringing party must have acted with willfulness and intent.

The TDRA provides the following exemptions to the act's protection of famous marks:

1. Any fair use of a famous mark by another person other than as a designation of source for the person's own goods or services, including for advertising or promotion that permits consumers to compare goods or services, or identifying and parodying, criticizing, or commenting upon the famous mark owner or the owner's goods or services.
2. All forms of news reporting and news commentary.
3. Any noncommercial use of a mark.[22]

Many cases have dealt with famous trademarks. In *Tiffany and Co. v. Costco Wholesale Corp.*, Tiffany claimed that Costco willfully used the generic

---

[19]*Id.* at § 1125(c)(1).
[20]*Id.* at § 1127.
[21]*Id.* at § 1125(c)(5).
[22]*Id.* at § 1125(c)(3).

term "tiffany style" ring to cause consumers to mistakenly believe that Costco was selling rings made by Tiffany & Co. Instead, Costco claimed they sold "Tiffany rings." Tiffany prevailed.[23]

The TTAB case of *Chanel, Inc. v. Jerzy Makarczyk* offers a useful list of factors for evaluating dilution cases.[24] In *Chanel*, the well-known luxury brand successfully sued to prevent use of the CHANEL mark in connection with real estate services. The board considered the following factors:

1. The plaintiff owns a famous mark that is distinctive.
2. The degree of the inherent or acquired distinctiveness of the famous mark
3. The extent to which the owner of the famous mark is engaged in exclusive use of the mark.
4. The degree of recognition of the famous mark.
5. Whether willingness exists.
6. Actual association between the famous mark and the diluting mark.

Dilution of a famous trademark also takes place on the Internet. Cyberquatters and typo squatters imitate famous marks and their websites for financial gain. Cybersquatting involves registering domain names using the famous mark or a formulation that is similar to it in domain names. The cyberquatters then offers to sell the domain name to the mark's owner for a high fee (something called "parked sites"). Cyberquatters can also go further, for example by setting up a site that disparages the famous mark, demanding payment from the mark's owner to take down the site. Typo squatting draws Internet users to a website that uses a minute difference in spelling or design from that of the famous mark.

Policing domain names to uncover cyberquatters and typo squatters is a full-time job. I managed the enforcement of domain names for famous real estate brands for which infringements ran rampant. We would receive pages upon pages of reports from a watch services of worldwide trademarks

---

[23] *No. 13CV1041, 2015 WL 5231240 (S.D.N.Y. Sept. 8, 2015).*

Dike, Annie. "With This Ring, I Thee Infringe re: Tiffany's Jewelry Trademark." National Law Review, October 16, 2015. natlawreview.com/article/ring-i-thee-infringe-re-tiffany-s-jewelry-trademark.

[24] *Chanel, Inc. v Jerzy Marczak, 110 U.S.P.Q.2d 2013 (TTAB, 2014); see also Robert P. Feebler, Jr., Famous CHANEL Mark Diluted by CHANEL for Real Estate Services, INTA Bulletin 69, no. 15 (Aug. 15, 2014).*

or domain names and the volume of infringing occurrences was shocking. Cyberquatters not only were seeking to denigrate the famous real estate brands, they also sought to dilute and tarnish the brands' reputation by associating them with pornographic or disparaging material. In this case, we only policed core brands in the same or related classes, such as real estate, financial services, moving services, and online services for real estate and related services. I reviewed the reports, tagged any suspicious hits, and reported the most egregious to the attorney. We would review suspicious websites to determine if they were in fact infringers and not, for example, franchisees of the marks' owners. We would then send cease and desist letters drafted in a factual tone to the potential infringers. A reminder was docketed for four weeks after the letters were sent. If no response was received, another letter with a tougher tone was sent. If the matter could not be resolved through cease and desist letters, then a UDRP complaint had to be filed.

How to tackle a cybersquatter:

1. Review other domain names a registrant owns.
2. Send a mild cease and desist letter to the registrant.
3. Follow up in two weeks
4. Write another, more serious letter.
5. Follow up in a month.
6. Write a letter saying that litigation is forthcoming.
7. File a UDRP complaint.

Chapter Nine

Trade Dress

Trade dress is a type of trademark. It is defined as a symbol or device that is "total image and overall appearance" of a product, or the totality of its elements, and "may include features such as size, shape, color or color combinations, texture, graphics."[25] Trade dress is registrable as a trademark on the Principal Register if it is nonfunctional and distinctive as used on the products or services of the trademark.

Like other forms of trademarks, the trade dress must function as a trademark if it is to be registered as a federal trademark. If there is any question regarding the registrability of the trade dress, then the Examiner customarily considers the description of goods or services, the drawing, and the specimen to obtain a clear picture of the totality of the trade dress.

Trade dress includes two forms: product design and product packaging. Product design cannot be inherently distinctive without evidence of acquired distinctiveness or secondary meaning. The trademark may be registrable on the Supplemental Register and after 5 years, it is entitled to be transferred to the Principal Register as a 2(f) registration because the PTO considers it to have acquired distinctiveness. The registration will have the added benefits from being on the Principal Register. Alternatively, if the trademark owner has another registration for the exact mark, it will be accepted or if the first use date and usage has been longstanding, it should be allowed.

If the trademark is trade dress is the product's packaging, then it is required to be nonfunctional and distinctive also; it may be inherently distinctive, but if functional, it will never under any circumstances be

---

[25] *Wal-Mart Stores, Inc. v. Samara Bros., 529 U.S. 205, 54 USPQ2d 1065 (2000).*

registrable. Trade dress filed as is 1(b) application cannot be refused until an allegment of use is filed. Under no circumstance, neither product design or product packaging is registrable if functional.

Functionality of Trade Dress

Trade dress that is functional cannot serve as a trademark. Mere trade dress functionality is an absolute bar to registration. A feature of trade dress is considered functional if it is "essential to the use or purpose of the article or if it affects the cost or quality of the article." Qualitex Co. v. Jacobson Products.[26]

The Functionality doctrine seeks to protect utilitarian product features be properly sought through a limited-duration utility patent, and not through the potentially, unlimited protection of a trademark registration. The reasoning behind this is that once the patent has expired, the invention enters the public domain where it is available to register new and improved version of the invention. The government also urgently aims to protect free competition in the marketplace.

The TTAB uses the following factors in *In re Morton-Norwich Products, Inc*[27] to figure out functionality of trade dress:

1. The existence or absence of a utility patent that discloses the utilitarian advantages of the design sought to be registered;
2. Advertising by the applicant that touts the utilitarian advantages of the design;
3. Facts pertaining to the availability of alternative designs; and
4. Whether the design results from a comparatively simple or inexpensive method of manufacture.

Considering the critical issue of functionality, the Examiner must show sufficient evidence in totality of the trade dress to support a 2(e) rejection that is a final one. 1202.02(a)(v)

---

[26] *514 U.S. 159 (1995).*
[27] *671 F.2d 1332, 1342, 218 USPQ 9, 17 (C.C.P.A. 1982).*

BNA's Intellectual Property Law Resource Center, United States Patents Quarterly article based on *Deere & Co. v. Fimco Inc.*[28] John Deere, the famous and well-known producer of agricultural and gardening machinery, claims exclusive rights to the colors green and yellow and seeks to dismiss the aesthetic functionality. *Aesthetic functionality considers other alternatives, and if none, the others are at a competitive disadvantage.* John Deere claimed exclusive right to the colors green and yellow, but Fimco stated that agricultural products tend to be green and yellow and felt that they were at a competitive disadvantage. In a prior case *Deere & Co. v. Farhan, Inc.*,[29] the court held that John Deere was aesthetically functional.

Utility Patents

Utility patents are new or improved versions of useful articles of manufacture. The existence of a valid utility patent is prima facie evidence that trade dress is functional. A client who seeks protection for functional trade dress should seek registration as a utility patent instead of trademark protection.

In *Apple Inc. v. Samsung Electronics Co.*,[30] Samsung argued that Apple's design of the iPhone was merely functional and, therefore, was not protectable. The court applied the following criteria for judging the functionality of trade dress:

1. Whether the design has a utilitarian advantage; or whether alternative designs are available;
2. Whether advertising or promotion has praised the advantages of utilitarian and functional advantages; and
3. Whether the design results from simple or inexpensive manufacturing.

In *TrafFix Devices, Inc. v. Mktg. Displays, Inc.*[31] the Supreme Court resolved a circuit split regarding the proper weight to be afforded a utility patent in the functionality determination, stating:

---

[28] *Deere & Co. v. Fimco.*
[29] *Deere & Co. v. Farhhand, Inc.*, 560 F.supp 85 (SD Iowa 1982).
[30] *Apple Inc. v. Samsung Electronics Co.*, *Appeal Nos. 2014-1335, 2015-1029 (Fed. Cir. May 18, 2015).*
[31] *Traffix Devices, Inc. v. Mktingdisplays, Inc.*, 532 U.S. 23 (2001).

A utility patent is compelling evidence that the features there claimed are functional. If trade dress protection is sought for those features the compelling evidence of functionality based on the earlier patent adds great weight to the statutory presumption that features are considered functional until proved otherwise by the party seeking trade dress protection. Where the expired patent claimed the features in question, one who seeks to establish trade dress protection must carry burden of showing that the feature is not functional.

Advertising Promotional or Explanatory Material

Advertising and promotional materials must be carefully worded to avoid any inference of a trade dress being functional. If an Office Action is issued rejecting the trademark because it is considered functional, the Examiner requests the applicant to provide materials from the applicant's website showing use of the trade dress, advertising, promotional, or explanatory material concerning the goods or services, particularly any material specifically related to the features embodied in the proposed mark.

Advertising is promoting a product or service. Touting the advantages of the product or services' strongpoints is part of normal advertising. Sometimes this can be "mere puffery" which is given little weight by examiners because it is so commonplace. A suggestion that a product's feature aids or is essential to the product's operation causes inferences that the feature is merely functional.

It is often difficult when reviewing advertising and promotional materials, as well as, the defined advantages of a particular product and its' overall functionality is a fine line that may pose potential problems if evidence of this kind is submitted to the PTO to support a response to office action rejection. This can be seen in *In re Becton, Dickinson & Co; AS Holdings, Inc. v. H & C Micro, Inc.*[32] In this case, it shows how an applicant often has promotional materials touting the utilitarian advantages of the product feature are mere "puffery" and, thus, entitled to little weight in the functionality analysis. Where the advertising statements clearly emphasize specific utilitarian features of the design claimed as a mark, the Board will reject such assertions of "puffery." The examiner usually will overlook a

---

[32] *107 USPQ2d 1829 (TTAB 2013).*

determination of puffery as evidence of functionality, or to disregard it for purposes of the analysis.

Distinctiveness

In re TrafFix Devices, Inc. v. Mktg. Displays[33] and *In re Morton-Norwich Prods., Inc.*[34] In order for trade dress to be registrable, it must be have acquired secondary meaning by: (1) ownership of a U.S. registration on the Principal Register of the same mark based on use in commerce under §1; (2) ownership of a U.S. registration on the Principal Register of the same mark for other goods or services based on a foreign registration under §44(e) or §66(a) affidavit or declaration of use in commerce has been accepted; or being registered on the Supplemental Register for a period of 5 years or having acquired secondary meaning without 2(f) due to enormous advertising and promotional budgets, surveys, and other related evidence. If the applicant establishes that the proposed mark serves as an identifier of secondary source, the matter is registrable on the Principal Register.

However, the Supplemental Register does not require that a trademark be distinctive. It may only be registrable on the Supplemental Register because it accepts marks that are not distinctive. Only trademarks that are now being used can register on the Supplemental Register. As stated previously, once a trademark has acquired distinctiveness, it is transferrable to the Principal Register. If the applicant, has extensive advertising, marketing, or promotional use so that the average consumer associates trademark with the applicant and the Examiner approves, then the mark will proceed to register without requiring a 2(f) claim.

Unlike product design, product packaging may be inherently distinctive. In[35] ("The attribution of inherent distinctiveness to certain … product packaging derives from the fact that the very purpose of … encasing [a product] in a distinctive packaging, is most often to identify the source of the products"). If the applicant is seeking registration of a trademark

---

[33] *532 U.S. 23 (2001).*
[34] *671 F.2d 1332, 1342, 218 USPQ 9, 17 (C.C.P.A. 1982).*
[35] *529 U.S. 205, 54 USPQ2d 1065 (2000).*

consisting of product packaging, the Examiner must assess its inherent distinctiveness. If it is lacking distinctiveness, registration on the Principal Register must be refused because the proposed mark is non-distinctive trade dress.

Product packaging that is inherently distinctive and nonfunctional is registrable on the Principal Register with no need for a 2(f) claim. Packaging design always requires secondary meaning to be registerable. To determine if an element has inherent distinctiveness, examiners apply the *Seabrook Foods, Inc. v. Barwell Foods, Ltd*[36] factors, which consider whether the proposed mark is:

1. a "common" basic shape or design;
2. unique or unusual in a field;
3. a mere refinement of a commonly adopted and well-known form of ornamentation for a class of goods viewed by the public as a dress or ornamentation for the goods; or
4. capable of creating a commercial impression distinct from the accompanying words.

One of the above factors is sufficient to establish inherent distinctiveness. If part of a mark is not distinctive, the application should disclaim that part.

Functional trade dress cannot serve as a trademark, if a feature of that trade dress is "essential to the use or purpose of the article or if it affects the cost or quality of the article."[37]

Trade dress is not to be confused with ornamentation. Ornamentation is a "decorative feature may include words, designs, slogans or trade dress."[38] A trademark that is merely ornamental only represents a design characteristic and does not function as a trademark since the ornamentation is not an indicator of source, does not function as a trademark and therefore, must be refused registration.

Trade dress must not be merely ornamental. For example, considering functionality issue for non-traditional marks, like color, or sound, *Deere &*

---

[36] *568 F.2d 1342, 1344, 196 USPQ 289, 291 (C.C.P.A. 1977).*
[37] *Wal-Mart Stores, Inc. v. Samara Bros., 529 U.S. 205, 54 USPQ2d 1065 (2000).*
[38] *TMEP October 2017, §1202.03.*

Co. v. Fimco[39] in which Deere & Co. was successful in forbidding Fimco to use the colors yellow and green on their lawn care products and *T-Mobile v. Aio Wireless*[40] for the magenta color. These cases are related because John Deere and T-Mobile prevailed in being able to use a color as trade dress.

The TMEP discusses ornamental matters in a registration context.

1. Ornamental matter that serves as an identifier of a "secondary source" is registrable on the Principal Register.
2. Ornamental matter that is neither inherently distinctive nor a secondary source indicator may be registered on the Principal Register under 2(f), if the applicant establishes that the subject matter has acquired distinctiveness as a mark in relation to the goods.
3. Ornamental matter that is neither inherently distinctive nor an indicator of secondary source, and has not acquired distinctiveness, but is capable of attaining trademark significance, may be registered on the Supplemental Register in applications filed under §1 or §44. Some matter is determined to be purely ornamental and, incapable of trademark significance and registrable on either the Principal Register or the Supplemental Register.[41]

The TMEP goes on to say that the examiner should consider the following factors to determine whether ornamental matter can be registered: (1) the commercial impression of the proposed mark; (2) the relevant practices of the trade; (3) secondary source; and (4) evidence of distinctiveness.[42]

Color marks are never inherently distinctive, and cannot be registered on the Principal Register without a showing of acquired distinctiveness under §2(f). Examples of trade dress that has acquired distinctiveness sufficient to be registered include Tiffany's use of blue, John Deere's use of green, and T-Mobile's claim to magenta.

---

[39] *Deere & Co. v. Fimco Inc.*, W.D. Ky., No. 15–105, October 13, 2017.
[40] Fung, Brian. *"Court says T-Mobile owns the color magenta,"* Washington Post, Feb. 10, 2014 *T-Mobile v. Aio Wireless (S.D. Texas 2013).*
[41] TMEP, §1202.03.
[42] *Id.*

Chapter Ten

Policing Trademarks

Policing your trademarks is extremely important to maintaining registrations over time and preventing loss of rights. It is imperative that trademark owners have active policing and enforcement policies in place to protect against potential infringement by third parties and risk of others petitioning to cancel the registration for nonuse. The established policing methods are reviewing the PTO's Official Gazette for weekly published marks, Internet searches, and global watch services.

The statutory period for abandonment is 3 years, so if a trademark is not used and there is no future attempt to resume use, the mark is cancelled. It is the responsibility of the owner of a trademark to protect and police those marks so that no threats or potential litigation will harm existing registrations. Internal and external enforcement is necessary to ensure the trademark continues to be distinctive and a source identifier of the source.

Most large corporations own thousands of trademarks in their portfolio, some of which are international trademarks. It is necessary for the registrant to monitor the trademarks, particularly house marks, core marks or famous marks. Other, less significant marks may be of short term use do not require the same policing and enforcement effort. Sometimes a trademark or slogan is registered for a specific event or program and after conclusion, the trademark is to be abandoned and never used again. Family marks, on the other hand, are very valuable assets providing a forceful presence in the industry amongst competitors. House marks, core marks or famous marks are afforded the most aggressive enforcement.

The Official Gazette has all published marks on that week from Class 1 to 45, single class and multiple classes; newly issued registrations. The trademark paralegal reviews the volume and tags any potential infringements or other risks to the client's trademarks. This is assuming that you are familiar with your trademark portfolio, if not, then refer to the master list. If you are enforcing a house mark or famous mark against trademark dilution or tarnishment, that requires the most aggressive and thorough policing. These marks should be enforced heavily due to their highest level of protection and value. The paralegal then prepares a memo to the attorney advising of the potential risk to the client's trademarks. If the attorney determines that there is significant risk, then further research may be needed to determine if an opposition should be commenced. For a registrant to oppose a trademark, the owner should have a good chance of prevailing. Evaluating the applicant's trademark portfolio and corporate status is a good place to begin. Then performing a search on the TTAB's filing database to learn about any oppositions they are involved in.

If added time is needed for research as to whether an opposition should be filed, an Extension of Time to File an Opposition is granted automatically upon request. Oftentimes, an extension of time to file a Notice of Opposition is filed to give the registrant ample time to research the matter. A sample Notice of Opposition is contained in the Appendix.

With widespread use of the Internet and social media, the domain names policing and enforcement against cyberquatters or typo squatters. Also, the Internet is a marketplace for counterfeiters using auction sites such as eBay and Amazon. Periodic Internet searches can uncover potential infringers of trademarks and domain names. Not only should you be guarding against any possible infringers, but also the willful party that is aiming to denigrate your trademark and business reputation.

With large, global portfolios, it is recommended that core marks in related classes have watch services set up using companies, such as Thomson Reuters or Corsearch. Paralegals customarily review voluminous pages of findings each week. The reports contain federal trademark filings, state trademark registrations, domain name registrations, common law marks, business and corporate names, like the results contained in a comprehensive search. Printouts of relevant pages are sent directly to the paralegal for review. The paralegal in turn advises the attorney of any potential problems, usually in the form of a memo. If a potential risk is uncovered, then a Cease and Desist letter is sent to the potential infringer and monitored. It is time well spent.

The priority for enforcement efforts are for direct competitors with marks for the same or similar goods and services; the same or similar marks in totally unrelated goods or services are not worrisome, unless the trademark is a famous trademark, then any instance of the mark being used should be aggressively enforced.

Monitoring responses received should be filed in a separate file. Follow-ups must be sent if no response if received. Also, it is advisable to create a data chart detailing all possible infringements.

These filings are made on the TTAB website. Often, the opposition never proceeds. The procedure for opposing a published trademark and documents involved in the matter are found on the TTAB website. A method of solving this problem is by adopting a side-by-side agreement with the adverse party which agrees to use only under set circumstances. Limiting the marks use geographically is another solution. If it is a pending application and the registration is well known, the applicant may decide to abandon the application or amend the mark.

If you are enforcing a house mark or famous mark against trademark dilution, these marks should be enforced heavily. The paralegal will provide the filing of the trademark that would cause damage to their registration and forward the report to the trademark attorney for review. If it is a potential infringement, then further research may be needed to determine if an opposition should be commenced. If additional time is needed for research as to whether an opposition should be filed, an Extension of Time to File an Opposition is filed automatically upon request. Oftentimes, an extension of time to file a Notice of Opposition is filed to give the registrant ample time to research the matter. A sample Notice of Opposition is contained in the Appendix.

The Anti-Cybersquatting Consumer Protection Act (ACPA)[43] authorizes the registrant of the trademark being infringed upon to litigate in federal court and obtaining a domain name transfer back to the trademark registrant. The burden of proof is on the registrant of the trademark or domain to establish:

- The registrant in bad faith seeks financial gain from the trademark
- Trademark must have been distinctive as of the date of the domain registration
- Domain name is identical or confusingly similar to the trademark, and
- Trademark must be distinctive and have a priority date over the cyberquatters.

---

[43]The Anti-Cybersquatting Consumer Protection Act (ACPA).

ICANN implemented the Uniform Domain Name Dispute Resolution Policy (hereinafter "UDRP"), to resolve domain name disputes. This policy advocates arbitration, rather than litigation.

Domain name is identical or confusingly similar to a trademark

- Owner lack rights or interest in the domain name that are legitimate
- The domain name is used in bad faith and registered for that purpose.

All three of these factors must be present for the Opposer to prevail. Remedy available is that the complainant will have the domain name transferred to him while cancellation of the ownership of the perpetrator.

Chapter Eleven

TTAB

The TTAB has jurisdiction over adversarial proceedings involving trademarks. It has jurisdiction over four types of proceedings:

1. *Ex parte* **proceedings** in which an applicant appeals an examiner's unfavorable decision in a final office action.
2. **Cancellation proceedings** in which a plaintiff seeks cancellation of an existing registration of a trademark on either register. Cancellation proceedings may be brought by "any person who believes that he is or will be damaged by the registration."
3. **Concurrent use proceedings,** in which the Board determines whether one or more applicants is entitled to a concurrent registration on the Principal Register, potentially contingent upon amendments the Board may require. Concurrent use proceedings are initiated by a statement in the initial application.

Notice of Opposition

Before registration on the Principal Register, a mark must be published in the Official Gazette for 30 days to allow registrants to determine if the mark would damage them and if they wish to oppose the mark's registration. Oppositions are initiated by filing a Notice of Opposition with the TTAB. A notice of opposition to an application based on §1 or §44 may be filed either on paper or electronically. The Notice of Opposition must include a concise statement of the reasons the opposer believes that its registration would be damaged by the registration of the opposed mark, and must state the grounds for opposition.

A Notice of Opposition must be filed within 30 days from the date of publication of the opposed mark in the Official Gazette. The opposer may request deadline extensions to allow further time for research. The first 30-day extension is automatically extended upon request.

Because a Notice of Opposition commences litigation, the registrant must promptly begin to research the opposer and the merits of the opposition. Research includes a portfolio audit and TTAB records review to determine how litigious the registrant is and find information about the applicant's nature of business and channels of trade. Consideration should be given to the opposer's reputation and famousness within the field. If the opposer is well-known or well-respected, the applicant may wish to concede to the opposition rather than go forward with possible litigation. Extensions are available to allow the applicant to complete its research.

Another option is the two owners agree to implement and execute a co-existence agreement. This occurs by limiting description of goods or services or geographic locations the product is being sold. If co-existence or concurrent use cannot be used, then Notice of Opposition is appropriate. An automatic extension may be filed and thereafter, for cause extensions not to exceed 24 months.

Petition to Cancel

Another adversarial proceeding is a Petition to Cancel an existing registration. These usually arise after an examiner issues an Office Action with a rejection based on 2(d) and the applicant seeks to cancel the conflicting registrations cited in the Office Action. The applicant must present evidence that the conflicting mark has not been in use for at least three years, or that the owner is no longer in business. The Petition must state the grounds for the Opposition and payment of the prescribed fee may be filed by any person who believes that he is or will be damaged or a likelihood of dilution by blurring or dilution by tarnishment by the registration of a mark on the principal register:

1. That defendant's mark so resembles a mark registered in the Office, or a mark or trade name previously used in the United States by another and not abandoned, as to be likely, when used on or in connection with

the goods or services of the defendant, to cause confusion, or to cause mistake, or to deceive.

2. The mark, when used on or in connection with the goods or services of the defendant, is merely descriptive or deceptively misdescriptive of them, or that defendant's mark is primarily geographically descriptive or primarily geographically deceptively misdescriptive of them; and that defendant's mark is primarily merely a surname.

3. The mark is geographically deceptive.

4. The mark disparages members of a particular group.

5. The mark consists of or comprises scandalous matter or that defendant's mark falsely suggests a connection with plaintiff's name or identity.

6. The mark of product design has not acquired distinctiveness.

7. No bona fide use of defendant's mark in commerce prior to the filing of the use-based application for its registration or have a bona fide intent to use the mark in connection with the identified goods/services as of the filing date of the application.

8. The registrant's mark is a mere background design that does not function as a mark separate and apart from the words displayed thereon.

9. Registrant was not, at the time of the filing of its application for registration the rightful owner of the registered mark.

10. The mark, consists of a particular color combination applied to its goods, is ornamental and has not become distinctive as an indication of the source of defendant's goods.

11. The registration has not been obtained has not been used as a trademark or service mark.

12. That defendant's mark has been abandoned due to nonuse or due to a course of conduct that has caused the mark to lose significance as an indication of source.

13. The mark consists of or comprises the name of a living individual without the individual's consent.

14. The trademark's is generic.

15. The mark would dilute the distinctive quality of plaintiff's famous mark.[44]

---

[44] *TTAB, Trademark Trial and Appeal Board Manual of Procedure, Section 309.03(c).*

Ex Parte Appeal

Ex parte proceedings are appeals of an examiner's final Office Action and the appeal is due within six months of the date of the final Office Action. Notices of Appeal should be filed electronically.

Chapter Twelve

Counterfeits

Widespread use of the Internet provides open field for counterfeiting of goods using trademarks that are identical or almost identical to genuine marks. Knockoffs sometimes introduce some slight deviation on the packaging that the average consumer might not recognize, such as misspelling the trademark or slightly modifying a logo. Knockoffs are intended to cause consumers to believe they are purchasing genuine products. Counterfeiters target famous trademarks in apparel, jewelry, handbags, pharmaceuticals, and electronics and most are made in Asia or Latin America. Fake goods are especially present on auction sites like eBay, Amazon, and Etsy, and are also sold at flea markets, by street vendors, and sometimes in retail stores. Counterfeiters are extremely cunning and proficient at deceiving the public. Trademark owners lose millions of dollars each year in sales and in costs associated with policing against counterfeiters.

Stringent policing of counterfeits needs to be in place and systemically executed by trained professionals. Cybersquatting—whereby fake domain names misguide consumers into mistakenly thinking that they are buying authentic goods—is another aspect of counterfeiting and may contribute to the problem. In both instances, the intent of the counterfeiter is to create a wave of business for a lesser quality product.

Inc. magazine contains an article, "What is the Most Counterfeited Item in the World The Answer Will Surprise You" by Helena Ball[45] states that luxury and famous brands are mostly targeted but the most counterfeited brand is Nike according the Organization for Economic

---

[45] Ball, Helena. "What is the Most Counterfeited Item in the World? The Answer Will Surprise You.," April 20, 2016.

Cooperation and Development (hereinafter OCED). "Counterfeiters take advantage of our trust in trademarks and brand names to undermine economies and endanger lives."

"With This Ring, I Thee Infringe re: Tiffany's Jewelry Trademark"[46] provides an excellent discussion of a case involving the famous luxury jeweler, Tiffany & Co. and the discount store, Costco. Tiffany sued Costco for deliberately misleading consumers that "tiffany setting" rings are "tiffany rings." "Tiffany setting" for rings is a very common setting for engagement rings. Although the Tiffany trademark was not, Costco faced charges of intentionally and willfully misleading consumers into believing that Costco was selling rings created by Tiffany & Co., the famous luxury jeweler, rather than the "tiffany setting" which describes the type of setting for the diamond.

Another famous trademark case is *Burberry Ltd. V. J.C. Penney Corp. et al*[47]. J.C. Penney is charged with trademark infringement, counterfeiting, false designation of origin, and trademark dilution against Burberry's famous plaid design on the same type of products. J.C. Penney has offered for sale in their department store and sold fake outerwear with the plaid design. Burberry is a high-end luxury, famous, well-known brand selling their products and owning their trademark for over 100 years. J.C. Penney's customers are considered frugal, so it is suggestible that they willfully infringed the product and seeked to profit from the goodwill of Burberry. The Defendant is accused of tarnishing the reputation of the Plaintiff by passing off its' goods to consumers. J.C. Penney was charged a huge fine for these charges.

One of the most highly counterfeited items in the marketplace is Nike.

---

[46] *"With This Ring, I Thee Infringe re: Tiffany's Jewelry Trademark" by Annie Dike, 2/9/2016".*
[47] *USDC, SD, NY 16-00932 (March 8, 2016).*

Chapter Thirteen

Corporate Transactions

Corporate transactions involve both intellectual property and corporate law matters. Intellectual property being trademarks, patents, and copyrights is a valuable intangible asset that often plays an important part of the commercial transactions, such sale of a company, mergers and acquisitions.

Any commercial transaction begins with a Letter of Intent. The purpose of the Letter of Intent is to recite the story of the transaction, to identify what documents are required, the parties involved and any guarantors. The first step for a paralegal preparing for a transaction is to carefully review the Letter of Intent to have a clear understanding of the transaction and the trademarks and entities involved. The next step is to highlight the required documents, corporate entities, or other guarantors and whether any documents need to be certified, as it requires extra time. The paralegal should use the Letter of Intent to prepare a list of closing documents with a chart to monitor each document's status.

The paralegal may also want to create a set of folders labeled with each of the categories on the closing checklist so hard copies of all due diligence items can be efficiently organized.

Due diligence of global intellectual property is important. Since this book focuses on trademark management, we will discuss only trademarks in the due diligence process. The purchaser needs to be confident that the entity is not acquiring a dead trademark as an asset. In any transaction involving trademarks, a thorough due diligence process must be performed prior to closing to ensure that there are no undisclosed debts or litigation, no technical problems with the registrations, and the transaction documents correctly describe the marks.

Due diligence regarding the trademarks seeks to ensure an accurate list of trademarks showing a clear representation of the company's active

intellectual property. A crucial step to take during due diligence is to identify trademarks that are active and those abandoned or expired or obsolete.
Any inactive trademarks should be brought to the attorney's attention to
determine which are to be deleted. A trademark is considered abandoned
after three years of nonuse and registrations are cancelled after five years
of nonuse.

It's also crucial to identify the trademark assets worldwide. In large
corporations, international trademarks exist. The list should include registered marks, pending registrations, trade names, trade dress, common law
marks, state trademarks, and foreign trademarks. Keep the U.S. trademarks
in a separate chart. Most of the time, the larger the corporation, the more
extensive intellectual property portfolio will be. Obtain marketing and
advertising materials to review use of the parties' brands, and identify the
parties' use of social media.

Trademarks typically are owned by the parent company in a corporate
structure. However, in large organizations with many divisions trademarks
may be owned by subsidiaries as well. For example, a company might place
ownership of its brands in separate subsidiaries, which also own the related
trademark registrations. For example, the company is TmIP Corp. with subsidiaries of ABC, DRA, MDS. An ownership search using the PTO's TESS
system would be formatted as follows: *ow, as = TmIp or ABC or DRA or MDS.*

The ownership of each registration must be confirmed; one cannot rely
upon the seller's claim of ownership of trademarks. A trademark ownership search must be performed in each country where the transaction party
claims to have registrations. Confirm that the registrations correctly identify the registrant; if a registrant's name is not correct, the registration may
be void. Assignment databases should be searched as well to identify potential assignors or assignees of the marks. The details of each registration must
be carefully reviewed. Examine each registration's assignment history to
trace its ownership history. If a registration's ownership of record does not
reflect the complete chain of assignment the error will need to be corrected.

Ownership and assignment of trademarks and corporate entities are
very important. The Assignment Division of the PTO contains chain of
title of all trademarks that had ownership changes recorded. The trademarks owned by a division or brand may be the only one's relevant to
the transaction. Are there any international trademarks owned? They too
will need to be checked for validity. It is important to check to see if any

trademarks involved are still active and whether there is any deadline for filings within the next six months. The purchaser will need to be made aware of this so that no deadlines are overlooked.

On the corporate side, formation documents (Certificate of Incorporation and Articles of Organization), partnership agreements, foreign qualifications, and assumed business names. Certified copies of these documents will be required for closing but check if the foreign qualifications can be plain copies. Regarding corporate agreements, check the terms of each active agreement to verify that they correctly reflect the details of any trademark; if any changes are required, they will need to be incorporated into the post-transaction succession plan. Key in license agreements is a clause that seller to others must be the retention by the seller of approval over the quality of goods or services under the mark. Without this clause, the agreement is considered a "naked license agreement." Have the relevant license agreement up to date and if so, has it been recorded at the Assignment Branch of the PTO. Reviewing agreements for renewal terms is required. Are there any side-by-side or concurrent use agreements and to what extent any third parties are permitted to use the trademark?

In the context of transactional work, this type of due diligence checks whether the owner is the owner of record. Seller claims of assets are in fact accurate and intangible assets are patents, copyrights, domain names, and trademarks. "Due diligence" is the purchaser's investigation that the seller's representation of assets and financial status is accurate. A sample of these transactions are selling off a division of a company, Purchase and Sale, Acquisition or Merger or using intellectual property to guarantee a loan. These deals are very document intense with lengthy closing lists and often, more than one red weld containing documents required for the closing. In addition to the gathering of documents, dependent on the nature of the transaction, documents will need to be drafted. Closing lists and tracking charts to ensure that all required documents are received, particularly with respect to Good Standing Certificates and Certified copies of registrations. Tracking chart will provide the progress of the pre-closing phase of the transaction.

Also, be sure to check the PTO's assignment website and check chain of title. Recordal of assignment will need to be done. Sometimes the chain is long but it is critical because a trademark that does not show the proper owner, is useless. The next project is for the paralegal to determine if the company owns the trademarks, who is the owner, are they active, and very important, if there are any deadlines soon and if any foreign applications are to be filed claiming priority, then docketing a six-month deadline is important. Ownership is critical because a trademark must be filed by the correct owner or the application is void. In the case of large corporations, sometimes different trademarks are owned by parent and others by the subsidiary. Sometimes registrations are cancelled but still in use. Also, pending applications are sometimes abandoned at early stages or if a substantive office action issues and they do not expect to prevail. It is important to check your portfolio against the one the seller produces. Also, any pending applications under 1(b) that have not proven use and are not part of the existing business are deemed abandoned.[48]

Further, determining what litigation and potential litigation the company is involved with or any TTAB matters. What are the debts owed by the company?

The trademark list should highlight which registrations need to have certified copies, so that they can be requested from the PTO. It is easier to keep separate charts for patents and trademarks to eliminate confusion. Locate the original Certificates of Registration and pending applications with filing receipts and place them in a folder for safekeeping. The PTO charges a fee to replace lost certificates. It can be confirmed that four trademarks are active and note the deadlines. Before going to the expense of ordering certified copies of registration certificates, check the Letter of Intent to see if they are needed. If certain marks need to be assigned, it should be done immediately so at the very least, you would have application for recordal and executed assignment documents to confirm proper trademark ownership. Once you file to record the assignment at the PTO, they will stamp the cover sheet and return it to you.

Find out what marks are no longer needed so that they can be eliminated from the portfolio up front. Checking the status is very simple on the PTO website. In addition, and very important is to check on the TTAB side for the TTABVue to see if the company has any active oppositions or cancellations. The site enables you to retrieve all documents filed. Substitute Powers of Attorney need to be filed on all pending applications. Domain names need to be check on the domain registry. Have a list of all common-law trademarks that have not had applications filed but are in use.

---

[48]Lanham Act, 15 U.S.C. 1060; 37 C.F.R. 3.16.

Chapter Fourteen

Trademark Portfolio Audits

I t is good business practice to audit a master list of all worldwide trademarks owned or assigned by you each year. Let us focus on U.S. federal trademarks since this book is on U.S. trademark management. The paralegal creates a chart of all active U.S. trademarks that are owned or assigned to the company. Note that when a trademark is assigned to another party, that party becomes the owner, except if the trademark is being assigned as security interest to a bank or other financial institution. Newly filed trademarks are added and trademarks no longer active or desired are removed. This occurs frequently with respect to a company's logos.

Generally, it is good business practice to perform a trademark audit once a year to evaluate for general housekeeping, if all marks are being used; are the description of goods accurate or has the business expanded within the Class or expanded into different areas resulting in the need for additional applications covering those classes are required; the single most important trademark is a house mark, usually the name of the company, for example, Fujifilm or Conair and customarily the trademarks are cover all areas that the company does business in; are there any slogans that were needed short terms, e.g. for an event and once the event is over, the slogan is no longer needed; review designs or logos to insure that material alterations have not been made and if so, a fresh application needs to be filed and whether or not the design is being protected for color.

NICE CLASSIFICATION–11ᵗʰ Edition, Version 2017 International Classifications of Goods and Services

Class 1

Chemicals used in industry, science, and photography, as well as in agriculture, horticulture, and forestry; unprocessed artificial resins, unprocessed plastics; manures; fire extinguishing compositions; tempering and soldering preparations; chemical substances for preserving foodstuffs; tanning substances; adhesives used in industry.

Class 2

Paints, varnishes, lacquers; preservatives against rust and against deterioration of wood; colorants; mordants; raw natural resins; metals in foil and powder form for use in painting, decorating, printing and art.

Class 3

Bleaching preparations and other substances for laundry use; cleaning, polishing, scouring and abrasive preparations; non-medicated soaps; perfumery, essential oils, non-medicated cosmetics, non-medicated hair lotions; non-medicated dentifrices.

Class 4

Industrial oils and greases; lubricants; dust absorbing, wetting and binding compositions; fuels (including motor spirit) and illuminants; candles and wicks for lighting.

Class 5

Pharmaceuticals, medical and veterinary preparations; sanitary preparations for medical purposes; dietetic food and substances adapted for medical or veterinary use, food for babies; dietary supplements for humans and animals; plasters, materials for dressings; material for stopping teeth, dental wax; disinfectants; preparations for destroying vermin; fungicides, herbicides.

Class 6

Common metals and their alloys, ores; metal materials for building and construction; transportable buildings of metal; non-electric cables and wires of common metal; small items of metal hardware; metal containers for storage or transport; safes.

- metals and ores used as chemicals in industry or scientific research for their chemical properties, for example, bauxite, mercury, antimony, alkaline and alkaline-earth metals (Cl. 1);
- metals in foil and powder form for use in painting, decorating, printing and art (Cl. 2);
- electric cables (Cl. 9) and non-electric cables and ropes, not of metal (Cl. 22);
- pipes being parts of sanitary installations (Cl. 11), flexible pipes, tubes, and hoses, not of metal (Cl. 17) and rigid pipes, not of metal
- (Cl. 19);
- cages for household pets (Cl. 21);
- certain goods made of common metals that are classified according to their function or purpose, for example, hand tools, hand operated (Cl. 8), paper clips (Cl. 16), furniture (Cl. 20), kitchen utensils (Cl. 21), household containers (Cl. 21).

Class 7

Machines and machine tools; motors and engines (except for land vehicles); machine coupling and transmission components (except for land vehicles); agricultural implements other than hand-operated; incubators for eggs; automatic vending machines.

Class 8

Hand tools and implements (hand-operated); cutlery; side arms; razors.

Class 9

Scientific, nautical, surveying, photographic, cinematographic, optical, weighing, measuring, signaling, checking (supervision), life-saving and teaching apparatus and instruments; apparatus and instruments for conducting, switching, transforming, accumulating, regulating or controlling electricity; apparatus for recording, transmission or reproduction of sound or images; magnetic data carriers, recording discs; compact discs, DVDs and other digital recording media; mechanisms for coin-operated apparatus; cash registers, calculating machines, data processing equipment, computers; computer software; fire-extinguishing apparatus.

Class 10

Surgical, medical, dental, and veterinary apparatus and instruments; artificial limbs, eyes, and teeth; orthopedic articles; suture materials; therapeutic and assistive devices adapted for the disabled; massage apparatus; apparatus, devices, and articles for nursing infants; sexual activity apparatus, devices, and articles.

Class 11

Apparatus for lighting, heating, steam generating, cooking, refrigerating, drying, ventilating, water supply and sanitary purposes.

Class 12

Vehicles; apparatus for locomotion by land, air, or water.

Class 13

Firearms; ammunition and projectiles; explosives; fireworks.

Class 14

Precious metals and their alloys; jewelry, precious and semi-precious stones; horological and chronometric instruments.

- jewelry, including imitation jewelry, for example, paste jewelry;
- cuff links, tie pins, tie clips;
- key rings, key chains, and charms therefor;
- jewelry charms;
- jewelry boxes;
- part parts for jewelry, clocks, and watches, for example, clasps and beads for jewelry, movements for clocks and watches, clock hands, watch springs, watch crystals.

Class 15

Musical instruments.

Class 16

Paper and cardboard; printed matter; bookbinding material; photographs; stationery and office requisites, except furniture; adhesives for stationery or household purposes; artists' and drawing materials; paintbrushes; instructional and teaching materials; plastic sheets, films, and bags for wrapping and packaging; printers' type, printing blocks.

Class 17

Unprocessed and semi-processed rubber, gutta-percha, gum, asbestos, mica, and substitutes for all these materials; plastics and resins in extruded form for use in manufacture; packing, stopping and insulating materials; flexible pipes, tubes, and hoses, not of metal.

Class 18

Leather and imitations of leather; animal skins and hides; luggage and carrying bags; umbrellas and parasols; walking sticks; whips, harness and saddlery; collars, leashes, and clothing for animals.

Class 19

Building materials (non-metallic); non-metallic rigid pipes for building; asphalt, pitch, and bitumen; non-metallic transportable buildings; monuments, not of metal.

Class 20

Furniture, mirrors, picture frames; containers, not of metal, for storage or transport; unworked or semi-worked bone, horn, whalebone, or mother-of-pearl; shells; meerschaum; yellow amber.

Class 21

Household or kitchen utensils and containers; combs and sponges; brushes, except paintbrushes; brush-making materials; articles for cleaning purposes; unworked or semi-worked glass, except building glass; glassware, porcelain, and earthenware.

Class 22

Ropes and string; nets; tents and tarpaulins; awnings of textile or synthetic materials; sails; sacks for the transport and storage of materials in bulk;

padding, cushioning, and stuffing materials, except of paper, cardboard, rubber, or plastics; raw fibrous textile materials and substitutes therefor.

Class 23

Yarns and threads, for textile use.

Class 24

Textiles and substitutes for textiles; household linen; curtains of textile or plastic.

Class 25

Clothing, footwear, headgear.

Class 26

Lace and embroidery, ribbons, and braid; buttons, hooks and eyes, pins, and needles; artificial flowers; hair decorations; false hair.

Class 27

Carpets, rugs, mats and matting, linoleum, and other materials for covering existing floors; wall hangings (non-textile).

Class 28

Games, toys, and playthings; video game apparatus; gymnastic and sporting articles; decorations for Christmas trees.

Class 29

Meat, fish, poultry, and game; meat extracts; preserved, frozen, dried, and cooked fruits and vegetables; jellies, jams, compotes; eggs; milk and milk products; edible oils and fats.

Class 30

Coffee, tea, cocoa, and artificial coffee; rice; tapioca and sago; flour and preparations made from cereals; bread, pastries, and confectionery; edible ices; sugar, honey, treacle; yeast, baking-powder; salt; mustard; vinegar, sauces (condiments); spices; ice.

Class 31

Raw and unprocessed agricultural, aqua cultural, horticultural and forestry products; raw and unprocessed grains and seeds; fresh fruits and vegetables, fresh herbs; natural plants and flowers; bulbs, seedlings, and seeds for planting; live animals; foodstuffs and beverages for animals; malt.

Class 32

Beers; mineral and aerated waters and other non-alcoholic beverages; fruit beverages and fruit juices; syrups and other preparations for making beverages.

Class 33

Alcoholic beverages (except beers).

Class 34

Tobacco; smokers' articles; matches.

Class 35

Advertising; business management; business administration; office functions.

Class 36

Insurance; financial affairs; monetary affairs; real estate affairs.

Class 37

Building construction; repair; installation services.

Class 38

Telecommunications.

Class 39

Transport; packaging and storage of goods; travel arrangement.

Class 40

Treatment of materials.

Class 41

Education; providing of training; entertainment; sporting and cultural activities.

Class 42

Scientific and technological services and research and design relating thereto; industrial analysis and research services; design and development of computer hardware and software.

Class 43

Services for giving food and drink; temporary accommodation.

Class 44

Medical services; veterinary services; hygienic and beauty care for human beings or animals; agriculture, horticulture, and forestry services.

Class 45

Legal services; security services for the physical protection of tangible property and individuals; personal and social services.

Trademark Application[49]

Trademark Application, Principal Register

SERIAL NUMBER	
MARK INFORMATION	
*MARK	
STANDARD CHARACTERS	YES
USPTO-GENERATED IMAGE	YES
LITERAL ELEMENT	
MARK STATEMENT	The mark consists of standard characters, without claim to any font, style, size, or color.
REGISTER	Principal
APPLICANT INFORMATION	
*OWNER OF MARK	
*STREET	
*CITY	
*STATE	
*COUNTRY	
*ZIP/POSTAL CODE	
PHONE	
FAX	
EMAIL ADDRESS	

---

[49]https://teas.uspto.gov/forms/bas/

TYPE	
STATE/COUNTRY OF INCORPORATION	
INTERNATIONAL CLASS	
*IDENTIFICATION	
FILING BASIS	
ACTIVE PRIOR REGISTRATION(S)	
NAME	
FIRM NAME	
STREET	
CITY	
STATE	
COUNTRY	
ZIP/POSTAL CODE	
PHONE	
FAX	
EMAIL ADDRESS	
AUTHORIZED TO COMMUNI-CATE VIA EMAIL	
OTHER APPOINTED ATTORNEY	
CORRESPONDENCE INFORMATION	
NAME	
FIRM NAME	
STREET	
CITY	
STATE	
COUNTRY	
ZIP/POSTAL CODE	
PHONE	
FAX	
*EMAIL ADDRESS	
*AUTHORIZED TO COMMUNI-CATE VIA EMAIL	

APPLICATION FILING OPTION	
NUMBER OF CLASSES	
FEE PER CLASS	
*TOTAL FEE DUE	
*TOTAL FEE PAID	
SIGNATURE	
SIGNATORY'S NAME	
SIGNATORY'S POSITION	
SIGNATORY'S PHONE NUMBER	
DATE SIGNED	

Office Action

Office Action

ISSUE/MAILING DATE: 1/28/2009

This Office action is in response to applicant's communication received on January 20, 2009, in which the applicant amended the identification of goods and claimed prior registrations. The amendment to the identification of goods has been accepted and added to the record. Upon further consideration, the assigned examining attorney has reviewed the referenced application and determined the following. Every attempt is made to address all relevant issues in the first examination of trademark applications. The examining attorney regrets any inconvenience to the applicant now.

Section 2(D) Refusal – Likelihood of Confusion

Registration of the applied-for mark is refused because of a likelihood of confusion with the mark in U.S. Registration Nos. The applicant has applied to register XXX for "Print substrate, namely, transparent, opaque and translucent films for use with ink jet printers."

The registered marks are:

Trademark Act Section 2(d) bars registration of an applied-for mark that so resembles a registered mark that it is likely that a potential consumer would be confused or mistaken or deceived as to the source of the goods and/or services of the applicant and registrant. See 15 U.S.C. §1052(d). The court in in re E. I. du Pont de Nemours & Co., 476 F.2d 1357, 177 USPQ 563 (C.C.P.A. 1973) listed the principal factors to be considered when determining whether there is a likelihood of confusion under Section 2(d). See TMEP §1207.01. However, not all the factors are

necessarily relevant or of equal weight, and any one factor may be dominant in each case, depending upon the evidence of record. In re Majestic
Distilling Co., 315 F.3d 1311, 1315, 65 USPQ2d 1201, 1204 (Fed. Cir.
2003); see in re E. I. du Pont, 476 F.2d at 1361–62, 177 USPQ at 567.

In this case, the following factors are the most relevant: similarity of the
marks, similarity of the goods and/or services, and similarity of trade channels of the goods and/or services. See In re Opus One, Inc., 60 USPQ2d
1812 (TTAB 2001); In re Dakin's Miniatures Inc., 59 USPQ2d 1593
(TTAB 1999); In re Azteca Rest. Enters., Inc., 50 USPQ2d 1209 (TTAB
1999); TMEP §1207.01 et seq.

Comparison of the Marks

In a likelihood of confusion determination, the marks are compared for sim-
ilarities in their appearance, sound, meaning or connotation and commercial
impression. In re E. I. du Pont de Nemours & Co., 476 F.2d 1357, 1361, 177
USPQ 563, 567 (C.C.P.A. 1973); TMEP §1207.01. Similarity in any one
of these elements may be sufficient to find a likelihood of confusion. In re
White Swan Ltd., 8 USPQ2d 1534, 1535 (TTAB 1988); In re Lamson Oil
Co., 6 USPQ2d 1041, 1043 (TTAB 1987); see TMEP §1207.01.

In the present case, applicant's mark XXXXXXXXX is similar to the
registered marks in sound, appearance, and connotation. All the marks
include the identical term "XXXX." Marks may be confusingly similar in
appearance where there are similar terms or phrases or similar parts of
terms or phrases appearing in both applicant's and registrant's mark. See
Crocker Nat'l Bank v. Canadian Imperial Bank of Commerce, 228 USPQ 689
(TTAB 1986), aff'd sub nom. Canadian Imperial Bank of Commerce v.
Wells Fargo Bank, Nat'l Ass'n, 811 F.2d 1490, 1 USPQ2d 1813 (Fed.
Cir. 1987) (COMMCASH and COMMUNICASH); In re Phillips-
Van Heusen Corp., 228 USPQ 949 (TTAB 1986) (21 CLUB and "21"
CLUB (stylized)); In re Corning Glass Works, 229 USPQ 65 (TTAB 1985)
(CONFIRM and CONFIRMCELLS); In re Collegian Sportswear Inc.,
224 USPQ 174 (TTAB 1984) (COLLEGIAN OF CALIFORNIA and
COLLEGIENNE); In re Pellerin Milnor Corp., 221 USPQ 558 (TTAB
1983) (MILTRON and MILLTRONICS); In re BASF A.G., 189 USPQ
424 (TTAB 1975) (LUTEXAL and LUTEX); TMEP §1207.01.

Overall, the marks have the same commercial impression.

Comparison of the Goods and/or Services

The goods and/or services of the parties need not be identical or directly competitive to find a likelihood of confusion. See Safety-Kleen Corp. v. Dresser Indus., Inc., 518 F.2d 1399, 1404, 186 USPQ 476, 480 (C.C.P.A. 1975); TMEP §1207.01(a). Rather, they need only be related in some manner, or the conditions surrounding their marketing are such that they would be encountered by the same purchasers under circumstances that would give rise to the mistaken belief that the goods and/or services come from a common source. In re Total Quality Group, Inc., 51 USPQ2d 1474, 1476 (TTAB 1999); TMEP §1207.01; see, e.g., On-line Careline Inc. v. Am. Online Inc., 229 F.3d 1080, 1086–87, 56 USPQ2d 1471, 1475–76 (Fed. Cir. 2000); In re Martin's Famous Pastry Shoppe, Inc., 748 F.2d 1565, 1566–68, 223 USPQ 1289, 1290 (Fed. Cir. 1984).

Applicant's "Print substrate, namely, transparent, opaque and translucent films for use with ink jet printers" are related to the registrant's goods and services because the goods and services are used in connection with photographic printing. Accordingly, the goods and services would be sold to the same class of purchasers and encountered under circumstances leading one to mistakenly believe the goods and services originate from the same source.

Since the marks are similar and the goods are related, there is a likelihood of confusion as to the source of the applicant's goods. Therefore, applicant's mark is not entitled to registration.

Although applicant's mark has been refused registration, applicant may respond to the refusal(s) by submitting evidence and arguments in support of registration.

Ownership of Cited Registrations

If the marks in the cited registrations have been assigned to applicant, applicant can provide evidence of ownership of the marks by satisfying one of the following:

1. Record the assignment with the Assignment Services Division of the Office and provide a written statement to the trademark examining attorney that the assignment has been duly recorded;

2. Submit copies of documents evidencing chain of title; or
3. Submit the following statement, verified with an affidavit or signed declaration under 37 C.F.R. §2.20: "Applicant is the owner of U.S. Registration Nos. XXXX and others."

TMEP §812; see 15 U.S.C. §1060; 37 C.F.R. §3.25, 3.73; TMEP §502.

Advisory – Ownership of Cited Registrations

Please note that any statement of ownership of the cited registrations must be verified with an affidavit of signed declaration under 37 C.F.R. §2.20.

Advisory – Unity of Control

Unity of control is presumed in instances where, absent contradictory evidence, one party owns all another entity, or substantially all another entity and asserts control over the activities of the other entity. Such ownership is established, for example, when one party owns all or substantially all the stock of another or when one party is a wholly owned subsidiary of another. TMEP §1201.07(a). If applicant asserts unity of control, applicant must provide a verified statement explaining the nature of the legal relationship between the parties. If neither party owns all or substantially all the other party, applicant must also provide a detailed written explanation and any documentary evidence showing the parties' "unity of control" over the nature and quality of the goods and/or services in connection with which the trademarks and/or service marks are used, and the parties' "unity of control" over the use of the trademarks and/or service marks. The explanation must be verified with an affidavit or signed declaration under 37 C.F.R. §2.20, 2.33. TMEP §502.01. However, if one party owns all the other entity, and there is no contradictory evidence of record, the written statement need not be verified. TMEP §1201.02.

Miscellaneous

If applicant has questions about its application or needs assistance in responding to this Office action, please telephone the assigned trademark examining attorney.

Appendix D

Statement of Use[50]

Statement of Use

The table below presents the data as entered.

Input Field	Entered
SERIAL NUMBER	
LAW OFFICE ASSIGNED	
EXTENSION OF USE	
MARK SECTION (current)	
MARK	
LITERAL ELEMENT	
STANDARD CHARACTERS	
USPTO-GENERATED IMAGE	
MARK STATEMENT	
MARK SECTION (proposed)	
MARK	
LITERAL ELEMENT	
STANDARD CHARACTERS	
USPTO-GENERATED IMAGE	
MARK STATEMENT	
OWNER SECTION	
NAME	
STREET	
CITY	

---

[50]https://teas.uspto.gov/au/

STATE	
ZIP/POSTAL CODE	
COUNTRY	United States
CORRESPONDENCE SECTION (current)	
NAME	
FIRM NAME	
STREET	
CITY	
STATE	
POSTAL CODE	
COUNTRY	
PHONE	
EMAIL	
AUTHORIZED TO COMMUNI-CATE VIA E-MAIL	
DOCKET/REFERENCE NUMBER	
CORRESPONDENCE SECTION (proposed)	
NAME	
FIRM NAME	
INTERNAL ADDRESS	
STREET	
CITY	
STATE	
POSTAL CODE	
COUNTRY	
PHONE	
EMAIL	
AUTHORIZED TO COMMUNI-CATE VIA E-MAIL	
DOCKET/REFERENCE NUMBER	
GOODS AND/OR SERVICES SECTION	
INTERNATIONAL CLASS	
CURRENT IDENTIFICATION	

GOODS OR SERVICES DELETED FROM THE APPLICATION	
GOODS OR SERVICES IN USE IN COMMERCE	
FIRST USE ANYWHERE DATE	
FIRST USE IN COMMERCE DATE	
SPECIMEN FILE NAME(S)	
ORIGINAL PDF FILE	
CONVERTED PDF FILE(S) (1 page)	
SPECIMEN DESCRIPTION	
REQUEST TO DIVIDE	
PAYMENT SECTION	
NUMBER OF CLASSES IN USE	
SUBTOTAL AMOUNT [ALLEGA-TION OF USE FEE]	
TOTAL AMOUNT	
DECLARATION SIGNATURE	
SIGNATORY'S NAME	
SIGNATORY'S POSITION	
DATE SIGNED	
SIGNATORY'S PHONE NUMBER	
FILING INFORMATION	
SUBMIT DATE	

Notice of Publication

Jul 8, 2015

NOTICE OF PUBLICATION

Serial NO.:   Mark: XYZ
International Class(es): 14   (STANDARD CHARACTER MARK)
Publication Date: Applicant:
Ju 28, 2015

The mark of the application identified appears to be entitled to registration. The mark Will, in accordance With Section 12(a) Of the Trademark Act Of 1946, as amended be published in the Official Gazette on the date indicated above for the purpose of opposition by any person Who believes he Will be damaged by the registration of the mark. If no opposition is filed within the time specified by Section 13(a) of the Statute or by rules 2.101 or 2.102 of the Trademark Rules the Commissioner of Patents and Trademarks may issue a notice of allowance pursuant to section 13(b) of the Statute.

Copies Of the trademark portion Of the Official Gazette containing the publication of the mark may be obtained from:

The Superintendent of Documents
U.S. Government Printing Office
PO Box 371954
Pittsburgh, PA 15250-7954
Phone: 202-512-1800

By direction of the Commissioner.

Notice of Allowance

NOTICE OF ALLOWANCE

ISSUE DATE:

Serial Number:

Mark:

No opposition was filed for this published application. The issue date of this Notice of Allowance establishes the due date for the filing of a Statement of Use or a Request for Extension of Time to file a Statement of Use (Extension Request). WARNING: A Statement of Use that meets all legal requirements must be filed before a registration certificate can issue. Please read below for important information regarding the applicant's pending six (6) month deadline.

SIX (6)-MONTH DEADLINE: Applicant has six (6) MONTHS from the Notice of Allowance issue date to file either:

Serial Number:

Mark:

Docket/Reference Number:

Owner:

Correspondence Address:

This application has the following bases, but not necessarily for all listed goods/services:

Section 1(a): NO   Section 1(b): YES   Section 44(e): NO
GOODS/SERVICES BY INTERNATIONAL CLASS
025 -

Request for Ex parte Reexamination

Address to:

Mail Stop *Ex Parte* Reexam   **Attorney**
Commissioner for Patents   **Docket No.:** _____
P.O. Box 1450
Alexandria, VA 22313-1450   **Date:** _____

1. ☐ This is a request for *ex parte* reexamination pursuant to 37 CFR 1.510 of patent number _____ issued _____. The request is made by:

   ☐ patent owner. ☐ third party requester.

2. ☐ The name and address of the person requesting reexamination is:

   _____

   _____

   _____

3. ☐ Requester asserts ☐ small entity status (37 CFR 1.27) or ☐ certifies micro entity status (37 CFR 1.29). Only a patent owner requester can certify micro entity status. Form PTO/SB/15A or B must be attached to certify micro entity status.

4. a. ☐ A check in the amount of $ _____ is enclosed to cover the reexamination fee, 37 CFR 1.20(c)(1);

   b. ☐ The Director is hereby authorized to charge the fee as set forth in 37 CFR 1.20(c)(1) to Deposit Account No. _____ ;

   c. ☐ Payment by credit card. Form PTO-2038 is attached; **or**

   d. ☐ Payment made via EFS-Web.

5. ☐ Any refund should be made by ☐ check or credit to Deposit Account No. _____. 37 CFR 1.26(c). If payment is made by credit card, refund must be to credit card account.

6. ☐ A copy of the patent to be reexamined having a double column format on one side of a separate paper is enclosed. 37 CFR 1.510(b)(4).

7. ☐ CD-ROM or CD-R in duplicate, Computer Program (Appendix) or large table
   ☐ Landscape Table on CD

8. ☐ Nucleotide and/or Amino Acid Sequence Submission *If applicable, items a. – c. are required.*
   a. ☐ Computer Readable Form (CRF)
   b. Specification Sequence Listing on:
      i. ☐ CD-ROM (2 copies) or CD-R (2 copies); **or**
      ii. ☐ paper
   c. ☐ Statements verifying identity of above copies

9. ☐ A copy of any disclaimer, certificate of correction or reexamination certificate issued in the patent is included.

10. ☐ Reexamination of claim(s) _____ is requested.

11. ☐ A copy of every patent or printed publication relied upon is submitted herewith including a listing thereof on Form PTO/SB/08, PTO-1449, or equivalent.

12. ☐ An English language translation of all necessary and pertinent non-English language patents and/or printed publications is included.

13. ☐ The attached detailed request includes at least the following items:
   a. A statement identifying each substantial new question of patentability based on prior patents and printed publications. 37 CFR 1.510(b)(1).
   b. An identification of every claim for which reexamination is requested, and a detailed explanation of the pertinency and manner of applying the cited art to every claim for which reexamination is requested. 37 CFR 1.510(b)(2).

14. ☐ A proposed amendment is included (only where the patent owner is the requester). 37 CFR 1.510(e).

15. ☐ It is certified that the statutory estoppel provisions of 35 U.S.C. 315(e)(1) or 35 U.S.C. 325(e)(1) do not prohibit requester from filing this *ex parte* reexamination request. 37 CFR 1.510(b)(6).

16. ☐ a. It is certified that a copy of this request (if filed by other than the patent owner) has been served in its entirety on the patent owner as provided in 37 CFR 1.33(c).
The name and address of the party served and the date of service are:

_____

_____

Date of Service: _____; **or**

☐ b. A duplicate copy is enclosed since service on patent owner was not possible. An explanation of the efforts made to serve patent owner **is attached**. See MPEP 2220.

_____

17. Correspondence Address: Direct all communication about the reexamination to:
☐ The address associated with Customer Number: [   ]

OR

☐ Firm or
Individual Name _____

Address

City	State	Zip
Country		
Telephone	Email	

Notice of Appeal

IN THE UNITED STATES PATENT AND TRADEMARK OFFICE
BEFORE THE TRADEMARK TRIAL AND APPEAL BOARD

Application Serial
No.
Applicant

Notice of Appeal

Notice is hereby given that XXXX appeals to the Trademark Trial and Appeal Board the refusal to register the mark depicted in Application Serial No.

The refusal to register has been appealed as to the following classes of goods/services:

Class 020. First Use: 0 First Use In Commerce: 0

All goods and services in the class are appealed, namely: Picture Frames

Class 021. First Use: 0 First Use In Commerce: 0

All goods and services in the class are appealed, namely: Mugs, tumblers, drinking bottles; trays for domestic purposes; coasters not of paper and other than table linen; leather coasters, plastic coasters

Respectfully submitted,

Combined Declaration of Use and Incontestability Under Sections 8 & 15[51]

Combined Declaration of Use and Incontestability Under Sections 8 & 15

REGISTRATION NUMBER	
REGISTRATION DATE	
SERIAL NUMBER	
MARK SECTION	
MARK	
OWNER SECTION (current)	
NAME	
STREET	
CITY	
COUNTRY	
OWNER SECTION (proposed)	
NAME	
STREET	
CITY	
COUNTRY	
ATTORNEY SECTION	
NAME	
FIRM NAME	
STREET	
CITY	
STATE	

[51]https://teas.uspto.gov/postreg/s08n15

ZIP/POSTAL CODE	
COUNTRY	
PHONE	
FAX	
DOCKET NUMBERS	
OTHER APPOINTED ATTORNEY(S)	
DOMESTIC REPRESENTATIVE SECTION	
NAME	
FIRM NAME	
STREET	
CITY	
STATE	
ZIP/POSTAL CODE	
COUNTRY	
PHONE	
FAX	
DESIGN MARK FILE NAME(S)	
GOODS AND/OR SERVICES SECTION	
INTERNATIONAL CLASS	
KEEP EXISTING GOODS AND/OR SERVICES	
SPECIMEN FILE NAME(S)	
SPECIMEN DESCRIPTION	
PAYMENT SECTION	
NUMBER OF CLASSES	1
NUMBER OF CLASSES PAID	1
SUBTOTAL AMOUNT	300
TOTAL AMOUNT	300
SIGNATURE SECTION	
SIGNATURE	
SIGNATORY NAME	
SIGNATORY DATE	
SIGNATORY POSITION	Applicant's Attorney
FILING INFORMATION	
SUBMIT DATE	Mon May 10 16:32:18 EDT 2004

Combined Declaration of Use and Incontestability Under Sections 8 & 15 To the Commissioner for Trademarks:

REGISTRATION NUMBER:
REGISTRATION DATE: 05/19/1998

MARK: .... (stylized and/or with design)

The owner ...., is using the mark in commerce on or in connection with the goods and /or services as follows:

For International Class 025, the owner is using or is using through a related company or licensee the mark in commerce on or in connection with all goods and/or services listed in the existing registration.

The owner is submitting one specimen for each class showing the mark as used in commerce on or in connection with any item in the class of listed goods and/or services, consisting of a(n) Hang tag. Specimen-1

The registrant hereby appoints .... to submit this Combined Declaration of Use and Incontestability Under Sections 8 & 15 on behalf of the registrant. The attorney docket/reference number is 978875.

The registrant hereby appoints .... as registrant's representative upon whom notice or process in the proceedings affecting the mark may be served.

A fee payment in the amount of $300 will be submitted with the form, representing payment for 1 class(es), plus any additional grace period fee, if necessary.

Declaration

The owner is using or is using through a related company or licensee the mark in commerce on or in connection with the goods/services identified above, as evidenced by the attached specimen(s) showing the mark as used in commerce. The mark has been in continuous use in commerce for five consecutive years after the date of registration, or the date of publication under Section 12(c), and is still in use in commerce on or in connection with all goods and/or services as identified above. There has been no final decision adverse to the owner's claim of ownership of such mark for such goods and/or services, or to the owner's right to register the same or to keep the same on the register; and there is no proceeding involving said rights pending and not disposed of either in the Patent and Trademark Office or in the courts.

The undersigned being hereby warned that willful false statements and the like are punishable by fine or imprisonment, or both, under 18 U.S.C. Section 1001, and that such willful false statements and the like may jeopardize the validity of this document, declares that he/she is properly authorized to execute this document on behalf of the Owner; and all statements made of his/her own knowledge are true and that all statements made on information and belief are believed to be true.

Declaration of Use and/or Excusable Nonuse/Application for Renewal of Registration of a Mark under Sections Combined 8 & 9[52]

Input Field	Entered
REGISTRATION NUMBER	
REGISTRATION DATE	
SERIAL NUMBER	
MARK SECTION	
MARK	
ATTORNEY SECTION (current)	
NAME	
FIRM NAME	
STREET	
CITY	
STATE	
POSTAL CODE	
COUNTRY	
ATTORNEY SECTION (proposed)	
NAME	
FIRM NAME	
STREET	
CITY	
STATE	
POSTAL CODE	

---

[52]https://teas.uspto.gov/postreg/s08n09

COUNTRY	
PHONE	
FAX	
EMAIL	
AUTHORIZED TO COMMUNI-CATE VIA E-MAIL	
DOCKET/REFERENCE NUMBER	
OTHER APPOINTED ATTORNEY	
CORRESPONDENCE SECTION (current)	
NAME	
FIRM NAME	
STREET	
CITY	
STATE	
POSTAL CODE	
COUNTRY	
CORRESPONDENCE SECTION (proposed)	
NAME	
FIRM NAME	
STREET	
CITY	
STATE	
POSTAL CODE	
COUNTRY	
PHONE	
FAX	
EMAIL	
AUTHORIZED TO COMMUNICATE VIA E-MAIL	Yes
DOCKET/REFERENCE NUMBER	
GOODS AND/OR SERVICES SECTION	
INTERNATIONAL CLASS	
GOODS OR SERVICES	
SPECIMEN FILE NAME(S)	
SPECIMEN DESCRIPTION	
INTERNATIONAL CLASS	

GOODS OR SERVICES	
SPECIMEN FILE NAME(S)	
SPECIMEN DESCRIPTION	
INTERNATIONAL CLASS	
GOODS OR SERVICES	
SPECIMEN FILE NAME(S)	
SPECIMEN DESCRIPTION	
OWNER SECTION (current)	
NAME	
CITY	
STATE	
ZIP/POSTAL CODE	
COUNTRY	
OWNER SECTION (proposed)	
NAME	
STREET	
CITY	
STATE	
ZIP/POSTAL CODE	
COUNTRY	
LEGAL ENTITY SECTION (current)	
TYPE	
STATE/COUNTRY OF INCORPORATION	
PAYMENT SECTION	
NUMBER OF CLASSES	
NUMBER OF CLASSES PAID	
SUBTOTAL AMOUNT	
TOTAL FEE PAID	
SIGNATURE SECTION	
SIGNATURE	
SIGNATORY'S NAME	
SIGNATORY'S POSITION	
DATE SIGNED	
SIGNATORY'S PHONE NUMBER	
PAYMENT METHOD	
SUBMIT DATE	

Closing Chart

Corporate	Required	Requested	Received
Certificate of Incorporation and all amendments			
Qualification to do business in any states			
Certified copy of good standing certificate from state of formation and each state where registered			
By-laws and any amendments			
Domain names			
Seller's corporate resolutions			
Officer's certificate			
Agreements			
License agreements			
Franchise agreement			
Work for hire agreement			
Concurrent use agreements			
Co-existing agreement			
Nondisclosure agreement			
Agreements not to compete			

Trademark List for Closing

Trademarks	Serial No./ Reg. No.	Status	Certified Copies	Received
ABC	**11,111,111**	**Registration**	**Needed**	
XYZ	**22,222,222**	**Registration**	**Needed**	
CCC	33,333,333	Statement of Use due 6/12/16	Not needed	
CAC	**44,334,100**	**Registration Renewal due 6/1/16**	**Needed**	
ZAZA and Design	**555,555,55**	**Registered, Section 8 & 15 due 4/14/16**	**Needed**	
XXX logo	666,666,666	Statement of Use due 6/1/16	Not needed	
AGE	777,777,777	Filing Receipt received	Not needed	
ZOO	**88,888,888**	**Registered; Renewal due 5/1/16**	**Needed**	
WHERE THE MAGIC BEGINS	99,999,999	Cancelled 3/3/2005	Not needed	

Closing List[53]

DUE DILIGENCE

a) Corporate Documents.

- Certificate of Incorporation, Articles of Organization, DBAs and all amendments
- Bylaws, and all amendments
- The Company's organizational chart
- The Company's list of shareholders and number of shares held by each
- Certificate of Good Standing from the Secretary of State of the state where the Company is incorporated
- Assumed names and their business certificates
- A description of the composite nature of business and identify competitors and possible foreword looking.
- Annual Reports for the last 3 years
- Joint venture agreements

b) Financial Information.

- Audited financial statements, auditor's reports for last 3 years.
- Auditor's letters and replies for the past five years
- A schedule of all indebtedness and contingent liabilities
- A schedule of inventory
- A schedule of accounts payable and receivable

---

[53] *Talley, Monica Riva. "Trademark Due Diligence in Corporate Transactions," Patent Trademark and Copyright Journal, October 3, 2014, available at https://www.bna.com/trademark-due-diligence-n17179895825/.*

c) Physical Assets.
  - A schedule of fixed assets and their locations
  - All U.C.C. filings
  - All leases of equipment

d) Real Estate.
  - A schedule of the Company's business locations
  - Copies of all real estate leases, deeds, mortgages, title policies, surveys, zoning approvals, variances, or use permits

e) Intellectual Property.
  - A schedule of trademarks filed at the PTO, common law mark, trade names owned or assigned to the Seller
  - Name all famous trademarks and derivatives thereof.
  - Schedule of trademarks filed as CTMs and worldwide applications or registrations.
  - Consulting agreements, patent agreements, licensing, work for hire, royalty, franchise, marketing, and assignments of intellectual property (patents, trademarks, domain names, business names, and copyrights)
  - Any patent and trademark clearance reports and legal opinions
  - Any oppositions, cancellations, concurrent use proceedings or litigation occurred or is expected to occur for the Seller
  - A schedule of pending and active patents
  - A schedule of copyrights
  - Domain names
  - A description of important technical know-how
  - A description of methods used to protect trade secrets and know-how
  - Claims, actual or threatened by or against the Company regarding intellectual property or corporate matters.

f) Employees and Employee Benefits.
  - A list of employees including positions, current salaries, salaries, bonuses paid during last 3 years.
  - Employment, consulting, nondisclosure, noncompetition agreements between the Company and any of its employees
  - Resumes of key employees
  - The Company's personnel handbook and employee benefits
  - Summary plan descriptions of qualified/nonqualified retirement plans

- Collective bargaining agreements
- Employee relations, disciplinary actions, actual or threatened litigation for alleged wrongful termination, harassment, and discrimination
- A description of worker's compensation claim history
- A description of unemployment insurance claims history
- Copies of all stock option and stock purchase plans and a schedule of grants

g) Licenses and Permits.
  - Copies of any governmental licenses, permits, or consents
  - Any correspondence or documents relating to any proceedings of any regulatory agency

h) Environmental Issues.
  - Environmental audits, if any, for each property leased by the Company
  - A listing of hazardous substances used in the Company's operations
  - A description of the Company's disposal methods
  - A list of environmental permits and licenses
  - Correspondence, notices, files related to EPA, state, or local regulatory agencies
  - A list identifying and describing any environmental litigation or investigations

i) Taxes.
  - Federal, state, local, and foreign income tax returns for the last three years
  - Any audit and revenue agency reports
  - Any tax settlement documents for the last three years
  - Employment tax filings for three years
  - Excise tax filings for three years
  - Any tax liens

j) Material Contracts.
  - A schedule of all subsidiary, partnership, or joint venture relationships and obligations, and related agreements
  - Copies of all contracts between the Company and any officers, directors, shareholders
  - Loan agreements, bank financing arrangements, line of credit, or promissory notes which the Company is a party

- All security agreements, guarantees, mortgages, indentures, collateral pledges.
- Any distribution agreements, sales representative agreements, marketing agreements, and supply agreements
- Any letters of intent, term sheets, contracts, and closing transcripts from any mergers, acquisitions, or divestitures within last five years
- Any options and stock purchase agreements involving interests in other companies
- The Company's standard quote, purchase order, invoice, and warranty forms
- All nondisclosure or noncompetition agreements to which the Company is a party
- All other material contracts

k) Product or Service Lines.
- A list of all existing products or services and products or services under development
- List of new products
- Copies of all correspondence and reports related to any regulatory approvals or disapprovals of any Company's products or services
- A summary of all complaints or warranty claims
- A summary of results of all tests, evaluations, studies, surveys, and other data regarding existing products or services and products or services under development

l) Customer Information.
- A schedule of the Company's customers
- Any supply or service agreements
- A schedule of unfilled orders
- A list and explanation for any major customers lost over the last two years
- All surveys and market research reports relevant to the Company or its products or services
- The Company's current advertising programs, marketing plans, and budgets, and printed marketing materials
- A description of the Company's major competitors

m) Litigation.
- A schedule of all pending or threatened litigation and parties thereto
- Copies of insurance policies possibly providing coverage as to pending or threatened litigation

- Documents relating to any injunctions, consent decrees, or settlements to which the Company is a party
- A list of unsatisfied judgments

n) Insurance Coverage.
- A schedule and copies of the Company's general liability, personal and real property, product liability, errors and omissions, directors and officers, worker's compensation, and other insurance
- Company's insurance claims history for past three years

o) Professionals.
- A schedule of all law firms, accounting firms, consulting firms, and similar professionals engaged by the Company during past five years

p) Articles and Publicity.
- Copies of all articles and press releases relating to the Company within the past three years
- Articles of competitors
- Articles or promotional materials on new products

Lanham Act

Chapter 15 - Trademark Act of 1946, as Amended

Title I The Principal Register

§1 (15 U.S.C. §1051) Application for registration; verification

1. The owner of a trademark used in commerce may request registration of its trademark on the principal register hereby established by paying the prescribed fee and filing in the PTO an application and a verified statement, in such form as may be prescribed by the Director, and such number of specimens or facsimiles of the mark as used as may be required by the Director.
2. The application shall include specification of the applicant's domicile and citizenship, the date of the applicant's first use of the mark, the date of the applicant's first use of the mark in commerce, the goods in connection with which the mark is used, and a drawing of the mark.
3. The statement shall be verified by the applicant and specify that the person making the verification believes that he or she, or the juristic person in whose behalf he or she makes the verification, to be the owner of the mark sought to be registered; to the best of the verifier's knowledge and belief, the facts recited in the application are accurate; the mark is in use in commerce; and to the best of the verifier's knowledge and belief, no other person has the right to use such mark in commerce either in the identical form thereof or in such near resemblance thereto as to be likely, when used on or in connection with the goods of such other person, to cause confusion, or to cause mistake, or to deceive, except that, in the case of every application claiming concurrent use, the applicant shall—

(i)   state exceptions to the claim of exclusive use; and

(ii) shall specify, to the extent of the verifier's knowledge—

(I)   any concurrent use by others;

(II) the goods on areas in which each concurrent use exists;

(III) the periods of each use; and

(IV) the goods and area for which the applicant desires registration.

4.   The applicant shall comply with such rules or regulations as may be pre-scribed by the Director. The Director shall promulgate rules prescribing the requirements for the application and for obtaining a filing date herein.

1.   A person who has a bona fide intention, under circumstances showing the good faith of such person, to use a trademark in commerce may request registration of its trademark on the principal register hereby established by paying the prescribed fee and filing in the PTO an application and a verified statement, in such form as may be prescribed by the Director.

2.   The application shall include specification of the applicant's domicile and citizenship, the goods in connection with which the applicant has a bona fide intention to use the mark, and a drawing of the mark.

3.   The statement shall be verified by the applicant and specify that the person making the verification believes that he in whose behalf he or she makes the verification, to be entitled to use the mark in commerce; the applicant's bona fide intention to use the mark in commerce; to the best of the verifier's knowledge and belief, the facts recited in the application are accurate; and to the best of the verifier's knowledge and belief, no other person has the right to use such mark in com-merce either in the identical form thereof or in such near resemblance thereto as to be likely, when used on or in connection with the goods of such other person, to cause confusion, or to cause mistake, or to deceive. Except for applications filed no mark shall be registered until the applicant has met the requirements.

4.   The applicant shall comply with such rules or regulations as may be prescribed by the Director who shall promulgate rules prescribing the requirements for the application and for obtaining a filing date herein

(c) At any time during examination of an application an applicant who has made use of the mark in commerce may claim the benefits of such use for purposes of this chapter, by amending his or her application to bring it into conformity.

(d) 1. Within six months after the date on which the notice of allowance a mark is issued the applicant shall file in the PTO with such number of specimens or facsimiles of the mark as used in commerce as may be required by the Director and payment of the prescribed fee, a verified statement that the mark is in use in commerce and specifying the date of the applicant's first use of the mark in commerce and those goods or services specified in the notice of allowance on or in connection with which the mark is used in commerce. Subject to examination and acceptance of the statement of use, the mark shall be registered in the PTO a certificate of registration shall be issued for those goods or services recited in the statement of use for which the mark is entitled to registration, and notice of registration shall be published in the Official Gazette of PTO Such examination may include an examination of the factors Notice of registration shall specify the goods or services for which the mark is registered.

2. The Director shall extend, for one additional 6-month period, the time for filing the statement of use (1), upon written request of the applicant before the expiration of the 6-month period provided in paragraph (1). In addition to an extension the preceding sentence, the Director may, upon a showing of good cause by the applicant, further extend the time for filing the statement of use for periods aggregating not more than 24 months, pursuant to written request of the applicant made before the expiration of the last extension granted under this paragraph. Any request for an extension shall be accompanied by a verified statement that the applicant has a continued bona fide intention to use the mark in commerce and specifying those goods or services identified in the notice of allowance on or in connection with which the applicant has a continued bona fide intention to use the mark in commerce. Any request for an extension shall be accompanied by payment of the prescribed fee. The Director shall issue regulations setting forth guidelines for determining what constitutes good cause.

3. The Director shall notify any applicant who files a statement of use of the acceptance or refusal thereof and, if the statement of use is refused, the reasons for the refusal. An applicant may amend the statement of use.

4. The failure to timely file a verified statement of use or an extension request shall result in abandonment of the application, unless it can be shown to the satisfaction of the Director that the delay in responding

was unintentional, in which case the time for filing may be extended, but for a period not to exceed the period for filing a statement of use.

(e) If the applicant is not domiciled in the US the applicant may designate, by a document filed in the PTO the name and address of a person resident in the US on whom may be served notices or process in proceedings affecting the mark. Such notices or process may be served upon the person so designated by leaving with that person or mailing to that person a copy thereof at the address specified in the last designation so filed. If the person so designated cannot be found at the address given in the last designation, or if the registrant does not designate by a document filed in the PTO the name and address of a person resident in the US on whom may be served notices or process in proceedings affecting the mark, such notices or process may be served on the Director.

§2 (15 U.S.C. §1052) Trademark registrable on Principal Register; concurrent registration

No trademark by which the goods of the applicant may be distinguished from the goods of others shall be refused registration on the principal register on account of its nature unless it—

(a) Consists of or comprises immoral, deceptive, or scandalous matter; or matter which may disparage or falsely suggest a connection with persons, living or dead, institutions, beliefs, or national symbols, or bring them into contempt, or disrepute; or a geographical indication which, when used on or in connection with wines or spirits, identifies a place other than the origin of the goods and is first used on or in connection with wines or spirits by the applicant on or after one year after the date on which the WTO Agreement enters into force with respect to the US.

(b) Consists of or comprises the flag or coat of arms or other insignia of the US or of any State or municipality, or of any foreign nation, or any simulation thereof.

(c) Consists of or comprises a name, portrait, or signature identifying a particular living individual except by his written consent, or the name, signature, or portrait of a deceased President of the US during the life of his widow, except by the written consent of the widow.

(d) Consists of or comprises a mark which so resembles a mark registered in the PTO or a mark or trade name previously used in the US by another and not abandoned, as to be likely, when used on or in connection with the goods of the applicant, to cause confusion, or to cause mistake, or to deceive: *Provided,* if Director determines that confusion, mistake, or deception is not likely to result from the continued use by more than one person of the same or similar marks under conditions and limitations as to the mode or place of use of the marks or the goods on or in connection with which such marks are used, concurrent registrations may be issued to such persons when they have become entitled to use such marks as a result of their concurrent lawful use in commerce prior to (1) the earliest of the filing dates of the applications pending or of any registration; Use prior to the filing date of any pending application or a registration shall not be required when the owner of such application or registration consents to the grant of a concurrent registration to the applicant. Concurrent registrations may also be issued by the Director when a court of competent jurisdiction has finally determined that more than one person is entitled to use the same or similar marks in commerce. In issuing concurrent registrations, the Director shall prescribe conditions and limitations as to the mode or place of use of the mark or the goods on or in connection with which such mark is registered to the respective persons.

(e) Consists of a mark which, (1) when used on or in connection with the goods of the applicant is merely descriptive or deceptively misdescriptive of them, (2) when used on or in connection with the goods of the applicant is primarily geographically descriptive of them, except as indications of regional origin may be registrable when used on or in connection with the goods of the applicant is primarily geographically deceptively misdescriptive of them, (4) is primarily merely a surname, or (5) comprises any matter that, as a whole, is functional.

(f) Nothing shall prevent the registration of a mark used by the applicant which has become distinctive of the applicant's goods in commerce. The Director may accept as prima facie evidence that the mark has become distinctive, as used on or in connection with the applicant's goods in commerce, proof of substantially exclusive and continuous use thereof as a mark by the applicant in commerce for the five years before the date on which the claim of distinctiveness is made. Nothing in this section shall prevent the registration of a mark which, when used on or in connection with the goods of the applicant, is primarily geographically deceptively misdescriptive of them, and which became distinctive of the applicant's goods in commerce before the date of the enactment of the NAFTA A mark which would be likely to cause dilution by blurring or dilution by tarnishment may be refused registration only pursuant to a proceeding brought under section 13. A registration for a mark which would be likely to cause dilution by blurring or dilution by tarnishment under section 43(c), may be canceled.

§3 (15 U.S.C. §1053) Service marks registrable

Service marks shall be registrable, in the same manner and with the same effect as are trademarks, and when registered they shall be entitled to the protection in the case of trademarks. Applications and procedure under this section shall conform as nearly as practicable to those prescribed for the registration of trademarks.

§5 (15 U.S.C. §1055) Use by related companies

Where a registered mark or a mark sought to be registered is or may be used legitimately by related companies, such use shall inure to the benefit of the registrant or applicant for registration, and such use shall not affect the validity of such mark or of its registration, provided such mark is not used in such manner as to deceive the public. If first use of a mark by a person is controlled by the registrant or applicant for registration of the mark with respect to the nature and quality of the goods or services, such first use shall inure to the benefit of the registrant or applicant, as the case may be.

§6 (15 U.S.C. §1056) Disclaimers

(a) The Director may require the applicant to disclaim an unregistrable component of a mark otherwise registrable. An applicant may voluntarily disclaim a component of a mark sought to be registered.

(b) No disclaimer shall prejudice or affect the applicant's or registrant's rights then existing or thereafter arising in the disclaimed matter, or his right of registration on another application if the disclaimed matter be or shall have become distinctive of his goods or services.

§7 (15 U.S.C. §1057) Certificates of registration

(a) *Issuance and form.* Certificates of registration of marks registered upon the principal register shall be issued in the name of the US under the seal of the PTO and shall be signed by the Director or have his signature placed thereon, and a record thereof shall be kept in the PTO The registration shall reproduce the mark, and state that the mark is registered on the principal register under this chapter, the date of the first use of the mark, the date of the first use of the mark in commerce, the particular goods or services for which it is registered, the number and date of the registration, the term thereof, the date on which the application for registration was received in the PTO and any conditions and limitations that may be imposed in the registration.

(b) *Certificate as prima facie evidence.* A certificate of registration of a mark upon the principal register shall be prima facie evidence of the validity of the registered mark and of the registration of the mark, of the owner's ownership of the mark, and exclusive right to use the registered mark in commerce on or in connection with the goods or services specified in the certificate, subject to any conditions or limitations stated in the certificate.

(c) *Application to register mark considered constructive use.* Contingent on the registration of a mark on the principal register provided by this chapter, the filing of the application to register such mark shall constitute constructive use of the mark, conferring a right of priority, nationwide on or in connection with the goods or services specified in the registration against any other person except for a person whose mark has not been abandoned and who, prior to such filing—

has used the mark; has filed an application to register the mark which is pending or has resulted in registration of the mark; or has filed a foreign application to register the mark on the basis of which he or she has acquired a right of priority, and timely files an application to register the mark which is pending or has resulted in registration of the mark.

(d) *Issuance to assignee.* A certificate of registration of a mark may be issued to the assignee of the applicant, but the assignment must first be recorded in the PTO in case of change of ownership the Director shall, at the request of the owner and upon a proper showing and the payment of the prescribed fee, issue to such assignee a new certificate of registration of the said mark in the name of such assignee, and for the unexpired part of the original period.

(e) *Surrender, cancellation, or amendment by owner.* Upon application of the owner the Director may permit any registration to be surrendered for cancellation, and upon cancellation appropriate entry shall be made in the records of the PTO Upon application of the owner and payment of the prescribed fee, the Director for good cause may permit any registration to be amended or to be disclaimed in part: *Provided,* That the amendment or disclaimer does not alter materially the character of the mark. Appropriate entry shall be made in the records of the PTO and upon the certificate of registration.

(f) *Copies of PTO records as evidence.* Copies of any records, books, papers, or drawings belonging to the PTO relating to marks, and copies of registrations, when authenticated by the seal of the PTO and certified by the Director, or in his name by an employee of the Office duly designated by the Director, shall be evidence in all cases wherein the originals would be evidence; and any person making application therefor and paying the prescribed fee shall have such copies.

(g) *Correction of PTO mistake.* Whenever a material mistake in a registration, incurred through the fault of the PTO is clearly disclosed by the records of the Office a certificate stating the fact and nature of such mistake shall be issued without charge and recorded and a printed copy thereof shall be attached to each printed copy of the registration and such corrected registration shall thereafter have the same effect as if the same had been originally issued in such corrected form, or in the discretion of the Director a new certificate of registration may be issued without charge. All certificates of correction heretofore issued in accordance with the rules of the PTO and the registrations to which they are attached shall have the same force and effect as if such certificates and their issue had been specifically authorized by statute.

Whenever a mistake has been made in a registration and a showing has been made that such mistake occurred in good faith through the fault of the applicant, the Director is authorized to issue a certificate of correction or, in his discretion, a new certificate upon the payment of the prescribed fee: *Provided,* That the correction does not involve such changes in the registration as to require republication of the mark.

§8 (15 U.S.C. §1058) Duration, affidavits and fees

Each registration shall remain in force for 10 years, except that the registration of any mark shall be canceled by the Director unless the owner of the registration files in the PTO affidavits that meet the requirements within the following time periods:

1. Within the 1-year period immediately preceding the expiration of 6 years following the date of registration or the date of the publication.
2. Within the 1-year period immediately preceding the expiration of 10 years following the date of registration, and each successive 10-year period following the date of registration.
3. The owner may file the affidavit required under this section within the 6-month grace period immediately following the expiration of the periods with the fee

Requirements for Affidavit. The affidavit referred to in subsection (a) shall—state that the mark is in use in commerce; set forth the goods/services recited in the registration on or in connection with which the mark is in use in commerce; be accompanied by such number of specimens or facsimiles showing current use of the mark in commerce as may be required by the Director; and be accompanied by the fee prescribed by the Director; or set forth the goods and services recited in the registration on or in connection with which the mark is not in use in commerce; include a showing that any nonuse is due to special circumstances which excuse such nonuse and is not due to any intention to abandon the mark; and fee

(c) *Deficient Affidavit.* If any submission filed within the period including that the affidavit was not filed in the name of the owner of the registration, the deficiency may be corrected after the statutory time period, within the time prescribed after notification of the deficiency. Such submission shall be accompanied by the additional deficiency surcharge prescribed by the Director.

(d) *Notice of Requirement.* Special notice of the requirement for such affidavit shall be attached to each certificate of registration and notice of publication.

(e) *Notification of Acceptance or Refusal.* The Director shall notify any owner who files any affidavit required by this section of the Director's acceptance or refusal thereof and, in the case of a refusal, the reasons therefor.

(f) *Designation of Resident for Service of Process and Notices.* If the owner is not domiciled in the US the owner may designate, by a document filed in the PTO the name and address of a person resident in the US on whom may be served notices or process in proceedings affecting the mark. Such notices or process may be served upon the person so designated by leaving with that person or mailing to that person a copy thereof at the address specified in the last designation so filed. If the person so designated cannot be found at the last designated address, or if the owner does not designate by a document filed in the PTO the name and address of a person resident in the US on whom may be served notices or process in proceedings affecting the mark, such notices or process may be served on the Director.

§9 (15 U.S.C. §1059) Renewal of registration

(a) Each registration may be renewed for periods of 10 years at the end of each successive 10-year period following the date of registration upon payment of the prescribed fee and the filing of a written application, in such form as may be prescribed by the Director. Such application may be made at any time within 1 year before the end of each successive 10-year period for which the registration was issued or renewed, or it may be made within a grace period of 6 months after the end of each successive 10-year period, upon payment of a fee and surcharge prescribed therefor. If any application filed is deficient, the deficiency may be corrected within the time prescribed after notification of the deficiency, upon payment of a surcharge.

(b) If the Director refuses to renew the registration, the Director shall notify the registrant of the Director's refusal and the reasons therefor.

(c) If the registrant is not domiciled in the US the registrant may designate, by a document filed in the PTO the name and ad-dress of a person resident in the US on whom may be served notices or process in proceedings affecting the mark. Such notices or process may be served upon the person so designated by leaving with that person or mailing to that person a copy thereof at the address specified in the last designation so filed. If the person so designated cannot be found at the address given in the last designation, or if the registrant does not designate by a document filed in the PTO the name and address of a person resident in the US on whom may be served notices or process in proceedings affecting the mark, such notices or process may be served on the Director.

§10 (15 U.S.C. §1060) Assignment

A registered mark or a mark for which an application to register has been filed shall be assignable with the good will of the business in which the mark is used, or with that part of the good will of the business connected with the use of and symbolized by the mark. Notwithstanding the preceding sentence, no application to register a mark under 1(b) of this title shall be assignable prior to the filing of an amendment to bring the application into conformity with section 1(a) of this title or the filing of the verified statement of use except for an assignment to a successor to the business of the applicant, or portion to which the mark pertains, if that business is ongoing and existing.

In any assignment authorized by this section, it shall not be necessary to include the good will of the business connected with the use of and symbolized by any other mark used in the business or by the name or style under which the business is conducted.

Assignments shall be by instruments in writing duly executed. Acknowledgment shall be prima facie evidence of the execution of an assignment, and when recorded in the PTO the record shall be prima facie evidence of execution.

An assignment shall be void against any subsequent purchaser for valuable consideration without notice, unless the prescribed information reporting the assignment is recorded in the PTO within 3 months after the date of the assignment or prior to the subsequent purchase.

PTO shall maintain a record of information on assignments, in such form as may be prescribed by the Director.

An assignee not domiciled in the US may designate by a document filed in the PTO the name and address of a person resident in the US on whom may be served notices or process in proceedings affecting the mark. Such notices or process may be served upon the person so designated by leaving with that person or mailing to that person a copy thereof at the address specified in the last designation so filed. If the person so designated cannot be found at the address given in the last designation, or if the assignee does not designate by a document filed in the PTO the name and address of a person resident in the US on whom may be served notices or process in proceedings affecting the mark, such notices or process may be served upon the Director.

§11 (15 U.S.C. §1061) Acknowledgments and verifications

Acknowledgments and verifications required hereunder may be made before any person within the US authorized by law to administer oaths, or, when made in a foreign country, before any diplomatic or consular officer of the US or before any official authorized to administer oaths in the foreign country concerned whose authority shall be proved by a certificate of a diplomatic or consular officer of the US.

§12 (15 U.S.C. §1062) Publication

Upon the filing of an application for registration and payment of the prescribed fee, the Director shall refer the application to the examiner in charge of the registration of marks, who shall cause an examination to be made and if the applicant is entitled to registration, or would be entitled to registration upon the acceptance of the statement of use the Director shall cause the mark to be published in the Official Gazette of the PTO: *Provided,* That in the case of an applicant claiming concurrent use, or in the case of an application to be placed in an interference mark, if otherwise registrable, may be published subject to the determination of the rights of the parties to such proceedings.

If the applicant is found not entitled to registration, the examiner shall advise the applicant thereof and of the reason therefor. The applicant shall have a period of six months in which to reply or amend his application, which shall then be reexamined. This procedure may be repeated until (1) the examiner finally refuses registration of the mark or applicant fails for a period of six months to reply or amend or appeal, whereupon the application shall be deemed to have been abandoned, unless it can be shown to the satisfaction of the Director that the delay in responding was unintentional, whereupon such time may be extended.

§13 (15 U.S.C. §1063) Opposition

Any person who believes that he would be damaged by the registration of a mark upon the principal register, including the registration of any mark which would be likely to cause dilution by blurring or dilution by tarnishment may, upon payment of the prescribed fee, file an opposition in the PTO stating the grounds therefor, within thirty days after the publication of the mark sought to be registered. Upon written request prior to the expiration of the thirty-day period, the time for filing opposition shall be extended for an additional thirty days, and further extensions of time for filing opposition may be granted by the Director for good cause when requested prior to the expiration of an extension. The Director shall notify the applicant of each extension of the time for filing opposition. An opposition may be amended under such conditions as may be prescribed by the Director.

(b) Unless registration is successfully opposed—
1. a mark entitled to registration on the principal register based on an application filed under section 1(a) shall be registered in the PTO a certificate of registration shall be issued, and notice of the registration shall be published in the Official Gazette of the PTO or
2. a notice of allowance shall be issued to the applicant if the applicant applied for registration under section 1(b) of this title.

§14 (15 U.S.C. §1064) Cancellation

A petition to cancel a registration of a mark, stating the grounds relied upon, may, upon payment of the prescribed fee, be filed as follows by any person who believes that he is or will be damaged, including as a result of a likelihood of dilution by blurring or dilution by tarnishment by the registration of a mark on the principal register:

Within five years from the date of the registration of the mark. Within five years from the date of publication

At any time if the registered mark becomes the generic name for the goods or services, is functional, or has been abandoned, or its registration was obtained fraudulently If the registered mark becomes the generic name for less than all of the goods or services for which it is registered, a petition to cancel the registration for only those goods or services may be filed. A registered mark !shall not be deemed to be the generic name of goods or services solely because such mark is also used as a name of or to identify a unique product or service. The primary significance of the registered mark to the relevant public rather than purchaser motivation shall be the test for determining whether the registered mark has become the generic name of goods or services on or in connection with which it has been used.

§15 (15 U.S.C. §1065) Incontestability of right to use mark under certain conditions

Except on a ground for which application to cancel may be filed at any time except to the extent, to which the use of a mark registered on the principal register infringes a valid right acquired under the law of any State or Territory by use of a mark or trade name continuing from a date prior to the date of registration under this chapter of such registered mark, the right of the owner to use such registered mark in commerce for the goods or services on or in connection with which such registered mark has been in continuous use for five consecutive years subsequent to the date of such registration and is still in use in commerce, shall be incontestable: *Provided,* That—

1. there has been no final decision adverse to the owner's claim of ownership of such mark for such goods or services, or to the owner's right to register the same or to keep the same on the register; and
2. there is no proceeding involving said rights pending in the PTO or in a court and not finally disposed of; and
3. an affidavit is filed with the Director within one year after the expiration of any such five-year period setting forth those goods or services stated in the registration on or in connection with which such mark has been in continuous use for such five consecutive years and is still in use in commerce; and
4. no incontestable right shall be acquired in a mark which is the generic name for the goods or services or a portion thereof, for which it is registered.

Subject to the conditions above specified in this section, the incontestable right with reference to a mark registered under this chapter shall apply to a mark registered under the Act of March 3, 1881, or the Act of February 20, 1905, upon the filing of the required affidavit with the Director within one year after the expiration of any period of five consecutive years after the date of publication of a mark. The Director shall notify any registrant who files the above-prescribed affidavit of the filing thereof.

§16 (15 U.S.C. §1066) Interference

Upon petition showing extraordinary circumstances, the Director may declare that an interference exists when application is made for the registration of a mark which so resembles a mark previously registered by another, or for the registration of which another has previously made application, as to be likely when used on or in connection with the goods or services of the applicant to cause confusion or mistake or to deceive. No interference shall be declared between an application and the registration of a mark the right to the use of which has become incontestable.

§17 (15 U.S.C. §1067) Interference, opposition, and proceedings for concurrent use registration or for cancellation; notice; TTAB

(a) In every case of interference, opposition to registration, application to register as a lawful concurrent user, or application to cancel the registration of a mark, the Director shall give notice to all parties and shall direct a TTAB to determine and decide the respective rights of registration.

(b) TTAB shall include the Director, Deputy Director of the PTO the Commissioner for Trademarks, and administrative trademark judges who are appointed by the Director.

(c) Authority of the Secretary. The Secretary of Commerce may, in his or her discretion, deem the appointment of an administrative trademark judge who, before the date of the enactment of this subsection, held office pursuant to an appointment by the Director to take effect on the date on which the Director initially appointed the administrative trademark judge.

(d) Defense to Challenge of Appointment. It shall be a defense to a challenge to the appointment of an administrative trademark judge on the basis of the judge's having been originally appointed by the Director that the administrative trademark judge so appointed was acting as a de facto officer.

§18 (15 U.S.C. §1068) Refusal, cancellation, restriction of registration; concurrent use

Director may refuse to register the opposed mark, may cancel the registration, in whole or in part, may modify the application or registration by limiting the goods or services specified therein, may otherwise restrict or rectify with respect to the register the registration of a registered mark, may refuse to register any or all of several interfering marks, or may register the mark or marks for the person or persons entitled thereto, as the rights of the parties under this chapter may be established in the proceedings: Provided, That in the case of the registration of any mark based on concurrent use, the Director shall determine and fix the conditions and limitations no final judgment shall be entered in favor of an applicant under section 1(b) before the mark is registered, if such applicant cannot prevail without establishing constructive use.

§19 (15 U.S.C. §1069) Applicability, in inter partes proceeding, of equitable principles of laches, estoppel and acquiescence

In all inter partes proceedings equitable principles of laches, estoppel, and acquiescence, where applicable, may be considered and applied.

§20 (15 U.S.C. §1070) Appeal from examiner to TTAB

An appeal may be taken to the TTAB from any final decision of the examiner in charge of the registration of marks upon the payment of the prescribed fee.

§22 (15 U.S.C. §1072) Registration as notice

Registration of a mark on the principal register shall be constructive notice of the registrant's claim of ownership thereof.

Title II The Supplemental Register

§23 (15 U.S.C. §1091) Filing and registration for foreign use

In addition to the principal register, the Director shall keep a continuation of the register give effect to certain provisions of the convention for the protection of trademarks and commercial names, made and signed in the city of Buenos Aires, in the Argentine Republic, August 20, 1910, and for other purposes" to be called the supplemental register. All marks capable of distinguishing applicant's goods or services and not registrable on the principal register herein provided, except those declared to be unregistrable which are in lawful use in commerce by the owner thereof, on or in connection with any goods or services may be registered on the supplemental register upon the payment of the prescribed fee and compliance Nothing in this section shall prevent the registration on the supplemental register of a mark, capable of distinguishing the applicant's goods or services and not registrable on the principal register under this chapter, that is declared to be unregistrable if such mark has been in lawful use in commerce the owner thereof, on or in connection with any goods or services, since before December 8, 1993.

Upon the filing of an application for registration on the supplemental register and payment of the prescribed fee the Director shall refer the application to the examiner in charge of the registration of marks, who shall cause an examination to be made and if on such examination it shall appear that the applicant is entitled to registration, the registration shall be granted. If the applicant is found not entitled to registration

Re registration on the supplemental register, a mark may consist of any trademark, symbol, label, package, configuration of goods, name, word, slogan, phrase, surname, geographical name, numeral, device, any matter that as a whole is not functional, or any combination of any of the foregoing, but such mark must be capable of distinguishing the applicant's goods or services.

§24 (15 U.S.C. §1092) Cancellation

Marks for the supplemental register shall not be published for or be subject to opposition, but shall be published on registration in the Official Gazette of the PTO. Whenever any person believes that such person is or will be damaged by the registration of a mark on the supplemental register

1. for which the effective filing date is after the date on which such person's mark became famous and which would be likely to cause dilution by blurring or dilution by tarnishment or
2. on grounds other than dilution by blurring or dilution by tarnishment, such person may at any time, upon payment of the prescribed fee and the filing of a petition stating the ground, apply to the Director to cancel such registration.

The Director shall refer such application to the TTAB which shall give notice to the registrant. If it is found after a hearing before the Board that the registrant is not entitled to registration, or that the mark has been abandoned, the registration shall be canceled by the Director, no final judgment shall be entered in favor of an applicant under section 1(b) before the mark is registered, if such applicant cannot prevail without establishing constructive use.

§25 (15 U.S.C. §1093) Supplemental registration certificate

The certificates of registration for marks registered on the supplemental register shall be conspicuously different from certificates issued for marks registered on the principal register.

§27 (15 U.S.C. §1095) Principal registration not precluded by supplemental registration

Registration of a mark on the supplemental register, shall not preclude registration by the registrant on the principal register established by this chapter. Registration of a mark on the supplemental register shall not constitute an admission that the mark has not acquired distinctiveness.

Title III Notice of Registration

§29 (15 U.S.C. §1111) Notice of registration; display with mark; recovery of profits and damages in infringement suit

Registrant of a mark registered in the PTO may give notice that his mark is registered by displaying with the mark the words "Registered in U.S.

Patent and Trademark Office" or "Reg. U.S. Pat. & Tm. Off." or the letter R enclosed within a circle, thus ®; and in any suit for infringement under this chapter by such a registrant failing to give such notice of registration, no profits and no damages shall be recovered under the provisions of this chapter unless the defendant had actual notice of the registration.

§30 (15 U.S.C. §1112) Classification of goods and services; registration in plurality of classes

The Director may establish a classification of goods and services, for convenience of PTO administration, but not to limit or extend the applicant's or registrant's rights. The applicant may apply to register a mark for any or all of the goods or services on or in connection with which he or she is using or has a bona fide intention to use the mark in commerce: Provided, That if the Director by regulation permits the filing of an application for the registration of a mark for goods or services which fall within a plurality of classes, a fee equaling the sum of the fees for filing an application in each class shall be paid, and the Director may issue a single certificate of registration for such mark.

§31 (15 U.S.C. §1113) Fees

(a) The Director shall establish fees for the filing and processing of an application for the registration of a trademark or other mark and for all other services performed by and materials furnished by the PTO related to trademarks and other marks.

Title IV Remedies

§32 (15 U.S.C. §1114) Remedies; infringement; innocent infringers

1. Any person who shall, without the consent of the registrant—
(a) use in commerce any reproduction, counterfeit, copy, or colorable imitation of a registered mark in connection with the sale, offering for sale, distribution, or advertising of any goods or services on or in connection with which such use is likely to cause confusion, or to cause mistake, or to deceive; or

(b) reproduce, counterfeit, copy or colorably imitate a registered mark and apply reproduction, counterfeit, copy or colorable imitation to labels, signs, prints, packages, wrappers, receptacles or advertisements intended to be used in commerce upon or in connection with the sale, offering for sale, distribution, or advertising of goods or services on or in connection with which such use is likely to cause confusion, or to cause mistake, or to deceive, shall be liable in a civil action by the registrant for the remedies hereinafter provided. Registrant shall not be entitled to recover profits or damages unless the acts have been committed with knowledge that such imitation is intended to be used to cause confusion, or to cause mistake, or to deceive "any person" includes the US, all agencies and instrumentalities thereof, and all individuals, firms, corporations, or other persons acting for the US and with the authorization and consent of the United States, and any State, any instrumentality of a State, and any officer or employee of a State or instrumentality of a State acting in his or her official capacity. US, all agencies and instrumentalities thereof, and all individuals, firms, corporations, other persons acting for the US and with the authorization and consent of the US, and any State, and any such instrumentality, officer, or employee

2. Remedies given to the owner of a right infringed under this chapter or to a person bringing an action shall be limited as follows:

(A) Where an infringer or violator is engaged solely in the business of printing the mark or violating matter for others and establishes that he or she was an innocent infringer or innocent violator, the owner of the right infringed or person bringing the action shall be entitled as against such infringer or violator only to an injunction against future printing.

(B) Where the infringement or violation complained of is contained in or is part of paid advertising matter in a newspaper, magazine, or other similar periodical or in an electronic communication the remedies of the owner of the right infringed or person bringing the action of this title as against the publisher or distributor of such newspaper, magazine, or other similar periodical or electronic communication shall be limited to an injunction against the presentation of such advertising matter in future issues of such newspapers, magazines, or other similar periodicals or in future transmissions of such electronic communications. The limitations of this subparagraph shall apply only to innocent infringers and innocent violators.

(I) A domain name registrar, a domain name registry, or other domain name registration authority that takes any action affecting a domain name shall not be liable for monetary relief for injunctive relief, to any person for such action, regardless of whether the domain name is finally determined to infringe or dilute the mark.

(II) A domain name registrar, domain name registry, or other domain name registration authority may be subject to injunctive relief only if such registrar, registry, or other registration authority has—

(aa) not expeditiously deposited with a court, in which an action has been filed regarding the disposition of the domain name, documents sufficient for the court to establish the court's control and authority regarding the disposition of the registration and use of the domain name;

(bb) transferred, suspended, or otherwise modified the domain name during the pendency of the action, except upon order of the court; or

(cc) willfully failed to comply with any such court order.

(ii) An action of refusing to register, removing from registration, transferring, temporarily disabling, or permanently canceling a domain name—

(II) in the implementation of a reasonable policy by such registrar, registry, or authority prohibiting the registration of a domain name that is identical to, confusingly similar to, or dilutive of another's mark.

(iii) A domain name registrar, a domain name registry, or other domain name registration authority shall not be liable for damages under this section for the registration or maintenance of a domain name for another absent a showing of bad faith intent to profit from such registration or maintenance of the domain name.

(iv) If a registrar, registry, or other registration authority takes an action described under clause (ii) based on a knowing and material misrepresentation by any other person that a domain name is identical to, confusingly similar to, or dilutive of a mark, the person making the knowing and material misrepresentation shall be liable for any damages, including costs and attorney's fees, incurred by the domain name registrant as a result of such action. The court may also grant injunctive relief to the domain name registrant, including the reactivation of the domain name or the transfer of the domain name to the domain name registrant.

(v) A domain name registrant whose domain name has been suspended, disabled, or transferred may, upon notice to the mark owner, file a civil action to establish that the registration or use of the domain name by such registrant is not unlawful. The court may grant injunctive relief to the domain name registrant, including the reactivation of the domain name or transfer of the domain name to the domain name registrant.

(E) "violator" means a person who violates and the term "violating matter" means matter that is the subject of a violation.

§33 (15 U.S.C. §1115) Registration as evidence of right to exclusive use; defenses

(a) Any registration issued under the Act of March 3, 1881, or the Act of February 20, 1905, or of a mark registered on the principal register shall be admissible in evidence and shall be prima facie evidence of the validity of the registered mark and of the registration of the mark, of the registrant's ownership of the mark, and of the registrant's exclusive right to use the registered mark in commerce on or in connection with the goods or services specified in the registration subject to any conditions or limitations stated therein, but shall not preclude another person from proving any legal or equitable defense or defect which might have been asserted if such mark had not been registered.

(b) To the extent that the right to use the registered mark has become incontestable the registration shall be conclusive evidence of the validity of the registered mark and of the registration of the mark, of the registrant's ownership of the mark, and of the registrant's exclusive right to use the registered mark in commerce. Such conclusive evidence shall relate to the exclusive right to use the mark on or in connection with the goods or services specified in the affidavit filed or in the renewal application filed if the goods or services specified in the renewal are fewer in number, subject to any conditions or limitations in the registration or in such affidavit or renewal application. Such conclusive evidence of the right to use the registered mark shall be subject to proof of infringement and shall be subject to the following defenses or defects:

1. That the registration or the incontestable right to use the mark was obtained fraudulently; or
2. That the mark has been abandoned by the registrant; or
3. Registered mark is being used, by or with the permission of the registrant or a person in privity with the registrant, so as to misrepresent the source of the goods or services on or in connection with which the mark is used; or
4. That the use of the name, term, or device charged to be an infringement is a use, otherwise than as a mark, of the party's individual name in his own business, or of the individual name of anyone in privity with such party, or of a term or device which is descriptive of and used fairly and in good faith only to describe the goods or services of such party, or their geographic origin; or
5. That the mark whose use by a party is charged as an infringement was adopted without knowledge of the registrant's prior use and has been continuously used by such party or those in privity with him from a date prior to the date of constructive use of the mark the registration of the mark if the application for registration is filed before the effective date of the TLRA of 1988, or (C) publication of the registered mark provided that this defense or defect shall apply only for the area in which such continuous prior use is proved; or
6. That the mark whose use is charged as an infringement was registered and used prior to the registration or publication of the registered mark of the registrant, and not abandoned: Provided, that this defense or defect shall apply only for the area in which the mark was used prior to such registration or such publication of the registrant's mark; or the mark has been or is being used to violate the antitrust laws of the US; or the mark is functional; or equitable principles, including laches, estoppel, and acquiescence, are applicable.

TITLE V False Designations of Origin, False Descriptions, and Dilution Forbidden

(a) 1. Any person who, on or in connection with any goods or services, or any container for goods, uses in commerce any word, term, name, symbol, or device, or any combination thereof, or any false designation of origin, false or misleading description of fact, or false or misleading representation of fact, which—

(A) is likely to cause confusion, or to cause mistake, or to deceive as to the affiliation, connection, or association of such person with another person, or as to the origin, sponsorship, or approval of his or her goods, services, or commercial activities by another person, or

(B) in commercial advertising or promotion, misrepresents the nature, characteristics, qualities, or geographic origin of his or her or another person's goods, services, or commercial activities, shall be liable in a civil action by any person who believes that he or she is or is likely to be damaged by such act.

2. As used in this subsection, the term "any person" includes any State, instrumentality of a State or employee of a State or instrumentality of a State acting in his or her official capacity. Any State, and any such instrumentality, officer, or employee, shall be subject to the provisions of this chapter in the same manner and to the same extent as any nongovernmental entity.

3. In a civil action for trade dress infringement under this chapter for trade dress not registered on the principal register, the person who asserts trade dress protection has the burden of proving that the matter sought to be protected is not functional, shall be liable in a civil action by any person who believes that he or she is or is likely to be damaged by such act.

(b) Any goods marked or labeled in contravention of the provisions of this section shall not be imported into the US or admitted to entry at any customhouse of the US. The owner, importer, or consignee of goods refused entry at any customhouse under this section may have any recourse by protest or appeal that is given under the customs revenue laws or may have the remedy involving goods refused entry or seized.

(c) Dilution by Blurring; Dilution by Tarnishment.--

1. Injunctive relief.--Subject to the principles of equity, the owner of a famous mark that is distinctive, inherently or through acquired distinctiveness, shall be entitled to an injunction against another person who, at any time after the owner's mark has become famous, commences use of a mark or trade name in commerce that is likely to cause dilution by blurring or dilution by tarnishment of the famous mark,

regardless of the presence or absence of actual or likely confusion, of competition, or of actual economic injury.

A mark is famous if it is widely recognized by the general consuming public of the US as a designation of source of the goods or services of the mark's owner. In determining whether a mark possesses the requisite degree of recognition, the court may consider all relevant factors, including the following:

The duration, extent, and geographic reach of advertising and publicity of the mark, whether advertised or publicized by the owner or third parties.

The amount, volume, and geographic extent of sales of goods or services offered under the mark extent of actual recognition of the mark.

Whether the mark was registered on the principal register.

Dilution by blurring' is association arising from the similarity between a mark or trade name and a famous mark that impairs the distinctiveness of the famous mark. In determining whether a mark or trade name is likely to cause dilution by blurring, the court may consider all relevant factors, including the following:

(i) The degree of similarity between the mark or trade name and the famous mark.

(ii) The degree of inherent or acquired distinctiveness of the famous mark.

(iii) The extent to which the owner of the famous mark is engaging in substantially exclusive use of the mark.

(iv) The degree of recognition of the famous mark.

(v) Whether the user of the mark or trade name intended to create an association with the famous mark.

(vi) Any actual association between the mark or trade name and the famous mark.

(C) Dilution by tarnishment' is association arising from the similarity between a mark or trade name and a famous mark that harms the reputation of the famous mark.

3. Exclusions.--The following shall not be actionable as dilution by blurring or dilution by tarnishment Any fair use, including a nominative or descriptive fair use, or facilitation of such fair use, of a famous mark by another person other than as a designation of source for the person's own goods or services, including use in connection with-- advertising or promotion that permits consumers to compare goods or services; or identifying and parodying, criticizing, or commenting

upon the famous mark owner or the goods or services of the famous mark owner. All forms of news reporting and news commentary. Any noncommercial use of a mark.

4. Burden of proof.--In a civil action for trade dress dilution under this Act for trade dress not registered on the principal register, the person who asserts trade dress protection has the burden of proving that--the claimed trade dress, taken as a whole, is not functional and is famous; and if the claimed trade dress includes any mark or marks registered on the principal register, the unregistered matter, taken as a whole, is famous separate and apart from any fame of such registered marks.

5. Additional remedies.--owner of the famous mark shall be entitled to injunctive relief The owner of the famous mark shall also be entitled to the remedies if--

(A) the mark or trade name that is likely to cause dilution by blurring or dilution by tarnishment was first used in commerce by the person against whom the injunction is sought after the date of enactment of the TDRA of 2006; and

(i) by reason of dilution by blurring, the person against whom the injunction is sought willfully intended to trade on the recognition of the famous mark; or

(ii) by reason of dilution by tarnishment, the person against whom the injunction is sought willfully intended to harm the reputation of the famous mark.

6. Ownership of valid registration a complete bar to action.--The ownership by a person of a valid registration on the principal register under this Act shall be a complete bar to an action against that person, with respect to that mark, that--

(A) is brought by another person under the common law or a statute of a State; and

(b) (i) seeks to prevent dilution by blurring or dilution by tarnishment; or

(ii) asserts any claim of actual or likely damage or harm to the distinctiveness or reputation of a mark, label, or form of advertisement.

(A) A person shall be liable in a civil action by the owner of a mark, including a personal name which is protected as a mark under this section, if, without regard to the goods or services of the parties, that person—

(i) has a bad faith intent to profit from that mark, including a personal name which is protected as a mark under this section; and

(ii) registers, traffics in, or uses a domain name that— in the case of a mark that is distinctive at the time of registration of the domain name, is identical or confusingly similar to that mark;

in the case of a famous mark that is famous at the time of registration of the domain name, is identical or confusingly similar to or dilutive of that mark; or

(i) In determining whether a person has a bad faith intent a court may consider factors such as, but not limited to—

(I) the trademark or other intellectual property rights of the person, in the domain name;

(II) the extent to which the domain name consists of the legal name of the person or a name that is otherwise commonly used to identify that person;

(III) the person's prior use, if any, of the domain name in connection with the bona fide offering of any goods or services;

(IV) the person's bona fide noncommercial or fair use of the mark in a site accessible under the domain name;

(V) the person's intent to divert consumers from the mark owner's online location to a site accessible under the domain name that could harm the goodwill represented by the mark, either for commercial gain or with the intent to tarnish or disparage the mark, by creating a likelihood of confusion as to the source, sponsorship, affiliation, or endorsement of the site;

(VI) the person's offer to transfer, sell, or otherwise assign the domain name to the mark owner or any third party for financial gain without having used, or having an intent to use, the domain name in the bona fide offering of any goods or services, or the person's prior conduct indicating a pattern of such conduct;

(VII) the person's provision of material and misleading false contact information when applying for the registration of the domain name, the person's intentional failure to maintain accurate contact information, or the person's prior conduct indicating a pattern of such conduct;

(VIII) the person's registration or acquisition of multiple domain names which the person knows are identical or confusingly similar to marks of others that are distinctive at the time of registration of such domain names, or dilutive of famous marks of others that are famous at the time of registration of such domain names, without regard to the goods or services of the parties; and

(IX)   the extent to which the mark incorporated in the person's domain name registration is or is not distinctive and famous

(ii)   Bad faith intent shall not be found in any case in which the court determines that the person believed and had reasonable grounds to believe that the use of the domain name was a fair use or otherwise lawful.

(C)   In any civil action involving the registration, trafficking, or use of a domain name a court may order the forfeiture or cancellation of the domain name or the transfer of the domain name to the owner of the mark.

(D)   A person shall be liable for using a domain name only if that person is the domain name registrant or that registrant's authorized licensee.

(E)   "traffics in" refers to transactions that include, but are not limited to, sales, purchases, loans, pledges, licenses, exchanges of currency, and any other transfer for consideration or receipt in exchange for consideration.

2)   (A) The owner of a mark may file an in rem civil action against a domain name in the judicial district in which the domain name registrar, domain name registry, or other domain name authority that registered or assigned the domain name is located if—

(i)   the domain name violates any right of the owner of a mark registered in the PTA or protected and

(ii)   the court finds that the owner— is not able to obtain in personam jurisdiction over a person who would have been a defendant in a civil action or through due diligence was not able to find a person who would have been a defendant in a civil action by sending a notice of the alleged violation and intent to proceed to the registrant of the domain name at the postal and e-mail address provided by the registrant to the registrar; and

(bb)   publishing notice of the action as the court may direct promptly after filing the action.

(B)   The actions under subparagraph (A)(ii) shall constitute service of process.

(C)   In an in rem action under this paragraph, a domain name shall be deemed to have its situs in the judicial district in which—

(i) the domain name registrar, registry, or other domain name authority that registered or assigned the domain name is located; or

(ii) documents sufficient to establish control and authority regarding the disposition of the registration and use of the domain name are deposited with the court.

(D) (i) The remedies in an in rem action under this paragraph shall be limited to a court order for the forfeiture or cancellation of the domain name or the transfer of the domain name to the owner of the mark. Upon receipt of written notification of a filed, stamped copy of a complaint filed by the owner of a mark in a US district court under this paragraph, the domain name registrar, domain name registry, or other domain name authority shall—

(I) expeditiously deposit with the court documents sufficient to establish the court's control and authority regarding the disposition of the registration and use of the domain name to the court; and

(II) not transfer, suspend, or otherwise modify the domain name during the pendency of the action, except upon order of the court.

(ii) The domain name registrar or registry or other domain name authority shall not be liable for injunctive or monetary relief under this paragraph except in the case of bad faith or reckless disregard, which includes a willful failure to comply with any such court order.

3. The civil action and the in rem action and any remedy available under either such action, shall be in addition to any other civil action or remedy otherwise applicable.

4. The in rem jurisdiction shall be in addition to any other jurisdiction that otherwise exists, whether in rem or in personam.

Title VI Construction and Definitions

§45 (15 U.S.C. §1127)

Commerce. The word "commerce" means all commerce which may lawfully be regulated by Congress.

Principal Register, Supplemental Register. The term "principal register" refers to the register and the term "supplemental register" refers to the register.

Person, juristic person. The term "person" and any other word or term used to designate the applicant or other entitled to a benefit or privilege or rendered liable includes a juristic person as well as a natural person. The term "juristic person" includes a firm, corporation, union, association, or other organization capable of suing and being sued in a court of law.

The term "person" also includes the US any agency or instrumentality or any individual, firm, or corporation acting for the US and with the authorization and consent of the US any agency or instrumentality thereof, and any individual, firm, or corporation acting for the US and with the authorization and consent of the US shall be subject to the provisions of this chapter in the same manner and to the same extent as any nongovernmental entity.

Applicant, registrant. The terms "applicant" and "registrant" embrace the legal representatives, predecessors, successors and assigns of such applicant or registrant.

Director. The term "Director" means the Under Secretary of Commerce for Intellectual Property and Director of the PTO.

Related company. The term "related company" means any person whose use of a mark is controlled by the owner of the mark with respect to the nature and quality of the goods or services on or in connection with which the mark is used.

Trade name, commercial name. The terms "trade name" and "commercial name" mean any name used by a person to identify his or her business or vocation.

Trademark. The term "trademark" includes any word, name, symbol, or device, or any combination thereof used by a person, or which a person has a bona fide intention to use in commerce and applies to register on the principal register established by this chapter, to identify and distinguish his or her goods, including a unique product, from those manufactured or sold by others and to indicate the source of the goods, even if that source is unknown.

Service mark. The term "service mark" means any word, name, symbol, or device, or any combination thereof—used by a person, or which a person has a bona fide intention to use in commerce and applies to register on the principal register established by this chapter, to identify and distinguish the services of one person, including a unique service, from the services of others and to indicate the source of the services, even if that source is unknown. Titles, character names, and other distinctive features of radio or television programs may be registered as service marks notwithstanding that they, or the programs, may advertise the goods of the sponsor.

Mark. The term "mark" includes any trademark, service mark, collective mark, or certification mark.

Use in commerce. The term "use in commerce" means the bona fide use of a mark in the ordinary course of trade, and not made merely to reserve a right in a mark. For purposes of this chapter, a mark shall be deemed to be in use in commerce—

1. on goods when it is placed in any manner on the goods or their containers or the displays associated therewith or on the tags or labels affixed thereto, or if the nature of the goods makes such placement impracticable, then on documents associated with the goods or their sale, and

(B) the goods are sold or transported in commerce, and

2. on services when it is used or displayed in the sale or advertising of services and the services are rendered in commerce, or the services are rendered in more than one State or in the US and a foreign country and the person rendering the services is engaged in commerce in connection with the services.

Abandonment of mark. A mark shall be deemed to be "abandoned" if either of the following occurs:

1. When its use has been discontinued with intent not to resume such use. Intent not to resume may be inferred from circumstances. Nonuse for 3 consecutive years shall be prima facie evidence of abandonment. "Use" of a mark means the bona fide use of such mark made in the ordinary course of trade, and not made merely to reserve a right in a mark.

2. When any course of conduct of the owner, including acts of omission as well as commission, causes the mark to become the generic name for the goods or services on or in connection with which it is used or otherwise to lose its significance as a mark. Purchaser motivation shall not be a test for determining abandonment under this paragraph.

Colorable imitation. The term "colorable imitation" includes any mark which so resembles a registered mark as to be likely to cause confusion or mistake or to deceive.

Registered mark. The term "registered mark" means a mark registered in the PTO "marks registered in the Patent and Trademark Office" means registered marks.

Prior acts. The term "Act of March 3, 1881," "Act of February 20, 1905," or "Act of March 19, 1920," means the respective Act as amended.

Counterfeit. A "counterfeit" is a spurious mark which is identical with, or substantially indistinguishable from, a registered mark.

Domain name. The term "domain name" means any alphanumeric designation which is registered with or assigned by any domain name registrar, domain name registry, or other domain name registration authority as part of an electronic address on the Internet.

Internet. The term "Internet" has the meaning given that term in section 230(f)(1) of the Communications Act of 1934 (47 U.S.C. 230(f)(1)).

Singular and plural. Words used in the singular include the plural and vice versa.

Glossary of Trademark Terms

Abandonment occurs when a trademark has been discontinued with purpose and intent to not resume use. Abandonment can occur as of the result of an applicant failing to respond to an Office Action or submit a Statement of Use by the prescribed deadline.

Acquired distinctiveness arises in a mark after five years of continuous use in commerce. Marks with acquired distinctiveness may register on the Principal Register under Section 2(f).

Amendment to Allege Use is when the mark commences use prior to the issuance of the Notice of Allowance.

Anti-dilution statutes are laws that enable the owner of a famous mark to prevent tarnishment or blurring of distinctiveness of the mark through unauthorized use.

Applicant is the owner of a trademark seeking registration with the PTO.

Arbitrary mark is a word in English used as a mark for goods or services that are not related to the word.

Assignment is the legal transfer of ownership of property, including intellectual property and all related interests, including goodwill, from one owner to the assignee. A contract that assigns ownership of a registered trademark must be recorded with the Assignment Branch of the PTO and notice must be given to relevant examiners, if applicable.

Attorney of Record is the attorney or law firm that is responsible for prosecuting the application until registration is finalized. The attorney of record is an authorized signatory of all documents submitted to the PTO in connection with the prosecution.

Availability search or comprehensive search is an extensive search of the trademark database of the PTO and any other relevant countries, common law marks, business names, domain names, articles, and other related evidence to be reviewed for trademark clearance.

Bad faith is acting with intent to mislead or deceive or to neglect a duty or contractual obligation.

Blurring is a lessening or weakening of the distinctiveness or strength of a famous mark.

Brand is the persona of a product and/or service derived from the goodwill of the business, and the reputation, quality, and characteristics of goods.

Cancellation is the extinguishing or expunging of a trademark registration by the TTAB or a court. Cancellation of a mark removes all exclusive rights to use the mark.

Cease and desist letter is the first step in first step in stopping another party from using an infringing mark. It provides evidence of potential harm or infringement and demands that the infringer stop using the registrant's mark.

Certificate of Registration is the official document issued by the PTO granting registration of a trademark in connection with the specified goods or services. It is prima facie evidence of the owner's exclusive right to use the mark in commerce. It is valid for 10 years; renewable indefinitely.

Certification Mark indicates the quality or characteristics of the marked goods or services.

Channels of trade are the methods used to market and/or sell goods or services, and/or the target market to which they are sold.

Class is identified numerically from 1 to 45 per the Manual of Identification of Goods and Services.

Clearance search is the formal process through which a proposed mark is checked against existing marks to ensure that the proposed mark does not infringe upon the trademark rights of others.

Coined term is a term that has been made up, with no meaning or purpose other than serving as a trademark (e.g., KODAK for cameras; EXXON for petroleum). Coined marks receive the highest level of trademark protection. See fanciful mark.

Coexistence agreement or side-by-side agreement is entered into by and among two or more persons or entities owning similar marks on similar goods or services. The agreement provides that the parties agree that the marks can be used by all parties without any likelihood of confusion, allows the parties to set rules by which the marks can peacefully co-exist, such as geographic boundaries. Also, see concurrent use agreement.

Collective Mark is a trademark used by members of a cooperative, association, or another collective group or organization to indicate their association with that group (GIRL SCOUTS for Girl Scout cookies, AAA for American Automobile Association).

Color Mark is a trademark containing and claiming color as part of the mark.

Common law marks are trademarks that have not been registered with the PTO but nonetheless can be protected against infringement.

Composite Mark is a trademark made up of several components, such as a word or words and design, for example Nike's JUST DO IT!

Concurrent Registration is a registration awarded to different registrants of the same mark, modified to some extent so that they can successfully co-exist in the marketplace.

Confusingly similar (2(d)) is when two trademarks are the same or similar and cover the same or similar goods or services.

Constructive date is the date on which a trademark first was used or filed, creating priority rights to subsequent filers or users.

Corporate Name is the legal name under which a corporation or other legal entity conducts business. If it functions as a trademark, it may be registrable.

Counterfeit is an intentional effort to deceive consumers by using a spurious mark that is identical to or substantially indistinguishable from a registered mark. Also, a copy or imitation of a product, made to resemble the original, often marketed or sold under a spurious mark.

Cybersquatting is use of another's mark in a domain name with bad-faith intent to profit from it.

Declaration of Use is an attestation filed with the PTO that a registered mark is still in use in commerce for the identified goods or services, accompanied by a specimen of such use. Failure to timely file a declaration of use results in cancellation of the registration. It is filed between the fifth and sixth anniversary of the registration of the mark.

Descriptive mark is a mark that merely describes the quality or characteristics of the marked goods or services. Unless the mark acquires secondary meaning, it is not registrable on the Federal Register; the mark may be registered on the Supplemental Register and after five years can be amended to the Principal Register.

Design mark or logo is a trademark consisting solely of a drawing or design with no words.

Dilution is the fading and lessening of the value of a famous trademark by a similar mark, regardless of whether the similar mark is used in connection with goods or services that are competitive with those of the famous mark's owner, and regardless of any likelihood of confusion.

Disclaimer is a statement in an application that an exclusive right over certain words or a portion of a mark is not claimed in the registration (e.g., because it is merely descriptive).

Distinctive mark presents a unique commercial impression. See inherently distinctive; acquired distinctiveness.

Domain Names are alphanumeric designations that are registered with or assigned by a domain-name registrar as part of an electronic address on the Internet (URL). Typically consists of a top-level domain (TLD) or "suffix" (e.g., ".com," ".org," etc.) and a second-level domain (SLD) chosen by the owner of the website. For example, in INTA's URL, http://www.inta.org, the domain name is "interior."

Dominant portion of a mark is the strongest and principal part of the mark; it creates the power of the mark's commercial impression and is weighed more heavily when evaluating conflicts with other marks.

Due Diligence is a level of prudence, activity, or care properly to be expected from a reasonable and prudent person under circumstances, not measured by an absolute standard but determined under the facts of the situation. When adopting a new mark, the purpose of carrying out a due diligence exercise is to avoid infringing the rights of others.

Enforcement is the active effort a trademark owner undertakes to protect its rights in its trademarks to prevent infringement, tarnishment, or dilution. Enforcement activities include cease and desist letters, Official Gazette review, use of a watch service, infringement litigation, and other means to prevent others from registering confusingly similar marks or using them in the marketplace.

Examiner is the official attorney that decides whether a trademark is entitled to registration.

Ex parte appeal requests TTAB review of a final PTO office action.

Examination is an analysis carried out by a trademark registrar, such as the PTO, to determine the registrability of a mark.

Examiner's Amendment is a communication from a PTO examining attorney to an applicant advising that the application has been amended by the trademark office (e.g., to change the description of goods and services, or add a disclaimer). An examiner's amendment must be authorized by the applicant or applicant's attorney, often via telephone conversation or e-mail.

Express abandonment is an official letter from the owner of a registration to the PTO stating that the owner is expressly and actively seeking to abandon the mark.

Fair Use is a good faith use of another's mark to describe one's own goods or services. It is an affirmative defense to a claim of trademark infringement.

False Advertising is advertising that is misleading or incorrect.

Family of marks consists of multiple marks possessing a common feature, such as a common prefix (e.g., the "Mc" of McDonalds), owned by the same party. Marks that are part of a family of marks are stronger.

Famous Mark is a trademark that has acquired sufficient reputation or recognition to be entitled to additional protections against infringement.

Fanciful terms or "coined marks" are words that are not found in the dictionary that are fabricated with the sole purpose of being a trademark.

Federal Trademark Dilution Act of 1996 amended the Lanham Act (Section 43(c)) to create a cause of action for owners of famous marks to prevent third party uses of the mark that might tarnish the mark or blur its distinctiveness, whether the goods and services are related.

File History is the contents of a trademark's official filings and actions in a trademark office related to the prosecution of a trademark application.

Filing Basis is one of several statutory grounds permitting registration of a mark. The four filing bases are: (1) use of the mark in commerce; (2) bona fide intent to use the mark in commerce; (3) a claim of priority based on an earlier filed foreign application; and (4) registration of the mark in the applicant's country of origin.

Filing Date is the date that the application was received at the PTO. In the case of an ITU application it is the date of constructive use.

Generic – common name for a term, such as dish.

Geographically descriptive terms suggest that goods come from a country, city, or other location that is known as a source of products (e.g., "Champagne" for sparkling wines from the Champagne region of France).

Goodwill is the favorable reputation of a business or trademark.

House mark is the principal mark owned by a trademark owner covering a wide range of goods and services, usually a corporate name.

Incontestability is a benefit that may be granted to a U.S. federal trademark registration, after a certain time and under certain conditions, protecting it from challenge on grounds that the mark is confusingly like another mark, is functional, or lacks secondary meaning.

Infringement is a violation of the rights of a trademark with priority by another mark that is confusingly similar to the senior mark.

Inherently distinctive refers to a mark that is strongly connected in the minds of consumers with the manufacturer's products.

Intellectual property refers to patents, trademarks, copyright, and domain names consisting of intangible assets.

Intent-to-use application or 1(b) is a trademark application filed prior to use of the mark in commerce.

International Trademark Association (INTA) is an elite nonprofit trademark organization that publishes materials about global trademark law, and conducts meetings of trademark professionals for education and networking.

International Classification refers to an official international system governed by the Nice Agreement by which "goods" are grouped into 45 classes, generally sorted by the material from which the goods are made and/or the use to which the goods are put. "Services" are grouped into 11 classes, generally sorted by the type of service provided. The purpose of the system is to enable trademarks to be searched and compared for possible conflicts.

International Registration is a trademark registration obtained from the World Intellectual Property Organization (WIPO) pursuant to the Madrid Agreement and/or the Madrid Protocol.

JPG is one of the formats for digital image files (with the file-name extension ".jpg") widely used for attaching images to applications submitted electronically to trademark offices.

Knockoff is an intentional deception by a party imitating the trademark of another to derive benefit from it.

Lanham Act (Trademark Act of 1946) is the federal statute governing the registration and maintenance of marks in the United States, and providing causes of action for infringement, unfair competition, dilution, and cybersquatting.

Laudatory is used to describe terms incorporated in a trademark that attributes quality or excellence (e.g., "best" or "original"). A laudatory term is considered merely descriptive cannot be registered unless it has acquired distinctiveness.

Licensing is how the owner of a mark (the "licensor") gives permission to another party (the "licensee") to use the licensor's trademark under specified conditions that would otherwise constitute infringement.

Likelihood of Confusion is the criterion for infringement whereby consumers might be confused as to the source of goods or services sold using similar marks.

Madrid Protocol is the trademark treaty enacted in 1995 (in conjunction with the 1891 Madrid Agreement) enabling trademark owners to obtain a single International Registration that can extend protection to any country that has signed the Protocol by a single filing in one language, under one procedure, and with payment of one fee. The Madrid system is administered by the World Intellectual Property Organization (WIPO).

Trademark or Mark is any word, name, symbol, or device, or any combination thereof, used to identify the goods or services of one party and distinguish them from the goods or services of other parties, and to indicate the source of the goods or services.

Material alteration is a post-application change of a mark from that shown in the original application, such that re-publication would be required.

Merely descriptive terms describe the qualities, features, ingredients, purpose, or characteristics of a product or service. Merely descriptive terms are not inherently distinctive, and are ineligible for trademark protection unless they are shown to have acquired distinctiveness or secondary meaning.

Nice Agreement is an International treaty establishing a uniform classification system for products and/or services claimed in trademark applications.

Nontraditional trademarks are marks that consist of shapes, music, color, smells, or other things that do not fit into the traditional trademark framework.

Notice of Allowance is an official notification from the PTO that an application filed on an intent-to-use basis will be allowed for registration once the applicant files a timely and acceptable statement of use (SOU).

Notice of Appeal is the document filed by an applicant with the TTAB to prevent registration of a mark that would be damaging to their registration.

Notice of Opposition is a document filed with the TTAB indicating the beginning of an infringement matter.

Notice of Publication is an official notice from the PTO that a mark is ready to be published in the Official Gazette for opposition purposes.

Office Action is an official correspondence from the examiner at the PTO either requesting changes to an application or raising substantive objections.

Official Gazette is the PTO publication that publishes marks for opposition purposes and publishes renewals and changes to existing marks.

Opinion letter is a letter by the attorney analyzing a search report for registrability and legal risk for possible infringement or dilution.

Opposition is an objection to a trademark registration filed by a third party that believes that a mark (1) poses a likelihood of confusion with an existing mark, or is (2) merely descriptive, (3) generic, or (4) deceptive.

Paris Convention is the treaty for prosection of industrial property providing common rules among convention countries for administering and protecting intellectual property rights.

Patent is the exclusive right to make, use, or sell an invention with respect to devices or methods that are deemed useful, novel, and non-obvious.

Petition to Revive is filed by an applicant or registrant seeking to revive or reactivate an application or registration deemed by a trademark office to be abandoned or cancelled.

Policing is monitoring the marketplace for unauthorized or improper uses of a mark, and accordingly pursuing enforcement of one's rights.

Preliminary search or "knock out search" is performed to spot readily identifiable conflicts at the outset of a screening process. Often used to narrow a list of potential marks under consideration.

Principal Register is the sought-after protection of a trademark conferring the right of exclusive use of the trademark.

Priority Date determines who has superior rights as between two parties using the same mark for similar goods and/or services. In the United States, the priority date is generally the date a trademark was first used in commerce (but see constructive use). In most other countries, the priority date is the date of the first filing of a trademark application. See first-to-file rule.

Publication provides public notice of a trademark application to allow third parties an opportunity to challenge the application.

Puffery is when advertising is so obviously inflated that the claims are not believable.

R in a circle or ® is the required notice written as a superscript symbol to indicate that a trademark or service mark has been granted registration by a trademark office. It is notice to the world of the owner's exclusive right to use the mark.

Registered mark is a mark that has been registered by the PTO.

Registrable refers to marks that meet the standards for federal registration.

Registrant is the owner or assignee of a federal trademark registration.

Registration is a granting of formal recognition of rights in a mark by a trademark office.

Related goods and services are goods that are related to the service. For example, financial software and financial services, or cosmetics and retail stores or online services selling cosmetics.

Renewal is an extension of a trademark registration for an additional period of ten years upon filing Section 8 & 9 application with the PTO.

Secondary meaning or 2(f) arises when a mark is used in commerce so extensively, through advertising and other efforts to develop product awareness in the marketplace, that the mark acquires distinctiveness after five years of continued use. Secondary meaning and 2(f) are often used interchangeably.

Section 8 is an affidavit that must be filed during the sixth year after a mark has been registered, and again at the time of each renewal of registration, together with a specimen evidencing that the mark is still in use in commerce on the goods or services covered by the registration.

Section 9 is the renewal application that must be filed every 10 years at the anniversary of the first registration of the trademark with the PTO, and every 10 years thereafter.

Section 15 concerns incontestability, which may occur after five years of continuous use of the registration.

Service mark is a name, brand, logo, or combination thereof adopted or used to identify and distinguish the services of one manufacturer from that of another. Marks can be in black and white or color, and can also incorporate motion or sound.

Slogans are service marks made of several words that have a meaning in the English language. For example, Nike's JUST DO IT!

Statement of Use is the document required to be filed in connection with an intent-to-use application proving use of the trademark in commerce prior to registration.

Strong mark has acquired inherent distinctiveness or acquired distinctiveness, length of use, extent of advertising penetration, etc. Strong marks are given more protection from infringement.

Suggestive mark connotes an attribute or characteristic of the mark when used for the goods and services.

Supplemental Register is the lower protection of trademarks that are descriptive in nature but under 2(f) can be transferred to the Principal Register once registered for five years. The Supplemental Register does not require or allow publication for opposition purposes.

Surnames usually cannot be registered as a mark without demonstration of secondary meaning and use as a trademark.

Tarnishment is the weakening of the distinctiveness of a famous mark, usually through inappropriate or unflattering associations; also, a form of dilution.

TM (™) is the notation used to show that a mark is being used as a trademark, either under common law or subject to a pending application.

Trade Dress is the overall commercial impression of a product or service. It may include the design or configuration of a product, packaging of goods, and/or the decor or environment in which services are provided. It can consist of such elements as size, shape, color, etc., to the extent such elements are not functional.

Trademark is a name, brand, logo, or combination thereof adopted or used to identify and distinguish the goods of one manufacturer or seller from that of another. Marks can be in black and white or color, or include motion or sound.

Trademark Application and Registration Retrieval (TARR) is the PTO's searchable database of status information for federal trademark applications and registrations.

Trademark Document Retrieval (TDR) is a system on the PTO website for online retrieval of documents from the electronic case file for federal trademark applications and registrations.

Trademark Electronic Application System (TEAS) is the PTO's online electronic filing system for federal trademark applications and forms relating to prosecution of applications and maintenance of registrations.

Trademark Electronic Search System (TESS) is the PTO's online searchable database of active and inactive federal trademark applications and registrations.

Trademark investigation is a comprehensive research of a registrant. It considers the registrant's trademark portfolio and other intellectual property ownership, domain names, corporate status, general nature of business, financial position, debts, and business ventures. An investigation also identifies any potential or actual threats of litigation or actual litigation.

Trademark Search is a preliminary search performed on the PTO site or proprietary database attempting to "knock out" the mark if a potentially conflicting mark exists.

Trademark Trial and Appeal Board (TTAB) is a division of the PTO that handles adversarial actions such as ex parte appeals, concurrent use proceedings, oppositions, and petitions to cancel registrations.

Trade Name is used by a company in its business activities and may also be its corporate name. A trade name may or may not also be used as a mark.

Use is actual marketing of the trademark in interstate commerce in connection with goods or services that are available for sale.

U.S. Patent and Trademark Office (PTO) is the governing federal agency for the prosecution and enforcement of trademarks.

Watch service is a third party retained for monitoring the marketplace for unauthorized or improper uses of one's marks. See policing.

Weak mark is a mark that lacks distinctiveness.

CPSIA information can be obtained
at www.ICGtesting.com
Printed in the USA
BVHW091933240419
546410BV00012B/229/P